I would like to dedicate this book to my wonderful wife, Diana, who has been committed to me for over 18 years. Also my 2 daughters, Erika and Isabella, who teach me something every day about what is important in life.

A huge thank to my mother Julia, and my recently deceased father, Vernon, who laid the foundation for my life. I could always count on them to be there through my successes and failures.

Finally to Jerry Cellan, who 15 years ago showed me how God could change my life and make me a better husband, father, and person. I would not be where I am today without him taking the time to mentor me.

To Your Success,

Wayne Peterson

I've always wanted to write a book but wondered if anyone would want to read what I had to say. Looking at my 20 plus years in business I reflected on how little practical knowledge I was taught about building a business through my education. After the financial crisis in 2008, I committed myself to finding a way to help businesses succeed. The business failure rate is over 80% and the median income for a small business owner is around $50,000 per year. Considering the risks, the sleepless nights, the loneliness of running a business, this hardly seems worth it.

I started to reflect on the fact that most business owners are not business owners at all, they are self-employed. A big difference. A business owner owns something of value. A self-employed person is someone who is their own boss.

Building a business of value requires that you differentiate yourself from others in your industry. This is how you create value. How do you do this? You need to start with the fundamentals. Distinguish yourself from your competitors and define your target market. This book gives you the fundamentals for attracting customers, keeping them, and getting them to refer others to you.

My passion for helping business drove me to develop an E-Learning system that any business can afford. It comes with the tactics, as well as the marketing and sales strategies that I charge companies $40,000 for me to help them implement. The information is delivered in a paint by numbers format so that any business owner with a desire to succeed can follow.

To Your Success,

Wayne A. Peterson

P.S. *If you would like to arrange a free marketing and business assessment please send me an email at wayne@waynesincomegenerationacademy.com and I will be glad to get you started in the right direction.*

Use Goal Setting Effectively

✦ ✦ ✦

We've all heard about the power of setting goals. Everyone has surely seen statistics that connect goal setting to success in both your business life, and your personal life. I'm sure if I asked you today what your goals are, you could rattle off a few wants and hopes without thinking too long.

However, what most people do not realize is that the power of goal setting lies in writing goals down. Committing goals to paper and reviewing them regularly gives you a 95% higher chance of achieving your desired outcomes. Studies have shown that only three to five percent of people in the world have written goals – the same three to five percent who have achieved success in business and earned considerable wealth.

These studies have also found that by retirement, only four per cent of people in the world will have enough accumulated wealth to maintain their income level, and quality of life. As a business owner, it is essential that you develop a plan for your retirement, but it is equally essential that you develop a plan for your success.

This chapter focuses on the power of goal setting as part of your business success. We'll teach you to set SMART goals that are rooted in your own personal value system, and supporting techniques to achieve your goals faster.

WHAT ARE GOALS?

Goals are clear targets that are attached to a specific time frame and action plan; they focus your efforts, and drive your motivation in a clear direction. Goals are different from dreams in that they outline a plan of action, while dreams are a conceptual vision of your wish or desired outcome.

Goals require work; work on yourself, work on your business, and work for others. You cannot achieve a goal – no matter how badly you want it – without being prepared to make a considerable effort. If you are ready to invest your time and energy, goals will help you to:

- Realize a dream or wish for your personal or business life
- Make a change in your life – add positive, or remove negative
- Improve your skills and performance ability
- Start or change a habit – positive or negative

WHY SET GOALS?

As we've already reviewed, setting goals and committing them to paper is the most effective way to cultivate success. The most important reason to set a goal is **to attach a clear action plan to a desired outcome.**

Goals help focus our time and energy on one (or several) key outcomes at a time. Many business owners have hundreds of ideas whirring around in their heads at any one time, on top of daily responsibilities. By writing down and focusing on a few ideas at a time, you can prioritize and concentrate your efforts, avoid being stretched too thin, and produce greater results.

Since goals attach action to outcomes, goals can help to break down big dreams into manageable (and achievable) sections. Creating a multi-goal strategy will put a road map in place to help you get to your desired outcome. If your goal is to start a pizza business and make six figures a year, there are a number of smaller steps to achieve before you achieve your end result.

Success doesn't happen by itself. It is the result of consistent and committed action by an individual who is driven to achieve something. Success means something different for everyone, so creating goals is a personal endeavor. Goals can be large and small, personal and public, financial and spiritual. It is not the size of the goal that matters; what matters is that you write the goal down and commit to making the effort required to achieve it.

WHAT HAPPENS WHEN I ACHIEVE A GOAL?

You should congratulate yourself and your team, of course! By rewarding yourself and your team after every achievement, you not only train your mind to associate hard work with reward, but develop loyalty among your employees.

You should also ask yourself if your achievement can be taken to the next level, or if your goal can be stretched by building on the effort you have already made. The hardest thing to do in life is to maintain the status quo, typically we are either progressing or regressing. Consistently setting new and higher targets will lay the framework for constant improvement and personal and professional growth.

POWER OF POSITIVE THINKING

When was the last time you tuned into your internal stream of consciousness? What does the stream of thoughts that run through your mind sound like? Are they positive? Negative? Are they logical? Reasonable?

Positive thinking and healthy self-talk are the most important business tools you can ever cultivate; by programming a positive stream of subconscious thoughts into your mind, you can control your reality, and ultimately your goals. Think about someone you know who is constantly negative; someone who complains and whines and makes excuses for their unhappiness. How successful are they? How do their fears and doubts become reality in their world?

You are what you continuously believe about yourself and your environment. If you focus your mind on something in your mental world, it will nearly always manifest as reality in your physical world.

Positive thinking is a key part of setting goals. You won't achieve your goal until you believe that you can. You will achieve your goals faster when you believe in yourself, and the people around you who are helping to make your goal a reality.

Successful people are rooted in a strong belief system – belief in themselves, belief in the work they are doing, and belief in the people around them. They are motivated to improve and learn, but also confident in their existing skills and knowledge. Their positive attitude and energy is clearly felt in everything they do.

Ever notice how complainers usually surround themselves with other complainers? The same is true of positive thinkers. If you cultivate an upbeat and positive attitude, you will be surrounded by people who share your values and outlook on life.

Too often, people and our society subscribe to a continuous stream of negative chatter. The more you hear it, the more you'll believe it.

How many times have you heard?

- That's impossible.

- Don't even bother.

- It's already been done.

- We tried that, and it didn't work.

- You're too young.

- You're too old.

- You'll never get there.

- You'll never get that done.

- You can't do that.

Positive thinking and positive influences will provide the support you need to achieve your goals. Choose your friends and close colleagues wisely, and surround yourself with positive thinkers.

CREATING SMART GOALS

SMART goals are just that: smart. Whether you are setting goals for your personal life, your business, or with your employees, goals that have been developed with the SMART principle have a higher probability of being achieved.

The SMART Principle

1. Specific

Specific goals are clearer and easier to achieve than nonspecific goals. When writing down your goal, ask yourself the five "W" questions to narrow in on what exactly you are aiming for. Who? Where? What? When? Why?

For example, instead of a nonspecific goal like, "get in shape for the summer," a specific goal would be, "go to the gym three times a week and eat four serving of vegetables daily." The answers to the five "W" questions for each specific goal will empower you to answer the "How" question on what strategies and steps you will need to take to accomplish each goal.

2. Measurable

If you can't measure your goal, how will you know when you've achieved it? Measurable goals help you clearly see where you are, and where you want to be. You can see change happen as it happens.

Measurable goals can also be broken down and managed in smaller pieces. They make it easier to create an action plan or identify the steps required to achieve your goal. You can track your progress, revise your plan, and celebrate each small achievement. For example, instead of aiming to increase revenue in 2014, you can set out to increase revenue by 30% in the next 12 months, and celebrate each 10% along the way.

3. Achievable

Goals that are achievable have a higher chance of being realized. While it is important to think big, and dream big, too often people set goals that are simply beyond their capabilities and wind up disappointed. Goals can stretch you, but they should always be feasible to maintain your motivation and commitment.

For example, if you want to complete your first triathlon but you've never run a mile in your life, you would be setting a goal that was beyond your current capabilities. If you decided instead to train for a five mile race in six months, you would be setting an achievable goal.

4. Relevant

Relevant – or realistic – goals are goals that have a logical place in your life or your overall business strategy. The goal's action plan can be reasonably integrated into your life, with a realistic amount of effort.

For example, if your goal is to train to climb to base camp at Mount Everest within one year and you're about to launch a start-up business, you may need to question the relevance of your goal in the context of your current commitments.

5. Timely

It is essential for every goal to be attached to a time-frame – otherwise it is merely a dream. Check in to make sure that your time-frame is realistic - not too short, or too long. This will keep you motivated and committed to your action plan, and allow you to track your progress.

AUTOSUGGESTION + VISUALIZATION

Autosuggestion and visualization are two techniques that can assist you in achieving your goals. Some of the most well-known and successful people in the world use these techniques, and it is not coincidence that they are masters in their own fields of business and sport. A few of these people include:

+ Michael Phelps (Olympic Swimmer)

+ Andre Agassi (Tennis)

+ Donald Trump (Real Estate)

+ Wayne Gretzky (Hockey)

+ Bill Gates (Microsoft)

+ Walt Disney (Entertainment)

Of course, each of these people have a high degree of talent, ambition, intelligence and drive. However, to reach the top of their respective field, they have each used Autosuggestion and Visualization. I recommend reading the book "Think and Grow Rich" by Napoleon Hill.

Autosuggestion

Autosuggestion is your internal dialogue; the constant stream of thoughts and comments that flows through your mind, and impacts what you think about yourself and how you perceive situations.

Since you were a small child, this self-talk has been influenced by your experiences and has programmed your mind to think and react in certain ways. The good news is that you can reprogram your mind and customize your self-talk any way you like. That is the power of Autosuggestion.

To begin practicing Autosuggestion, make sure you are relaxed and open to trying the technique; an ideal time is just before bed, or when you have some time to sit quietly. Then, repeat positive affirmations to yourself about the ideal outcome. Top sports and business people will often practice just before a big game or meeting.

Some examples of positive self-talk or autosuggestion include:

+ I will lead my team to a victory tonight!

+ I will be relaxed and open to meeting people at the party tonight!

+ I will deliver a clear and impacting speech!

+ I will stop worrying and tackle this problem tomorrow!

+ I will stand up for my own ideas in the meeting!

+ I will remember everything I have studied for the test tomorrow!

Visualization

Visualization is a practice complementary to Autosuggestion. While you can repeat affirmations to yourself over and over, combining this practice with visualization is twice as powerful.

Visualization is exactly what it sounds like: repeatedly visualizing how something is going to happen in your mind's eye. Nearly everyone in sports practices this technique. It has been proven to enhance performance better than practice alone.

This technique can easily be applied to business. For example, prior to any presentation or meeting where you must speak, present or "perform." You can also visualize yourself being incredibly productive and effective in your office. Or, having a discussion with your spouse calmly and rationally.

Elements to think about during visualization:

- What does the room look like?

- What do the people in the room look like?

- What is their mood? How do they receive me?

- What image do I project?

- How do I look?

- How do I behave? What is my attitude?

- What is the outcome?

Define Your
Target Market

✦ ✦ ✦

WHAT IS A TARGET MARKET?

Many businesses can't answer the question: Who is your target market? They have often made the fatal assumption that everyone will want to purchase their product or service with the right marketing strategy.

A target market is simply the group of customers or clients who will purchase a specific product or service. This group of people all have something in common, often age, gender, income level, hobbies, or location.

Your target market, then, are the people who will buy your offering. This includes both existing and potential customers, all of whom are motivated to do one of three things:

- ✦ Fulfill a need
- ✦ Solve a problem
- ✦ Satisfy a desire

To build, maintain, and grow your business, you need to know who your customers are, what they do, what they like, and why they would buy your product or service. Getting this wrong – or not taking the time to get it right – will cost you time, money, and potentially the success of your business.

THE IMPORTANCE OF KNOWING YOUR TARGET MARKET

Knowledge and understanding of your target market is the keystone in the arch of your business. Without it, your product or service positioning, pricing, marketing strategy, and eventually, your business could very quickly fall apart.

If you don't intimately know your target market, you run the risk of making mistakes when it comes to establishing pricing, product mix, or service packages. Your marketing strategy will lack direction, and produce mediocre results at best. Even if your marketing message and unique selling proposition (USP) are clear, and your brochure is perfectly designed, it means nothing unless it arrives in the hands (or ears) of the right people.

Determining your target market takes time and careful diligence. While it often starts with a best guess, assumptions cannot be relied on and research is required to confirm original ideas. Your target market is not always your ideal market.

Once you build an understanding of who your target market is, keep up with your market research. Having your finger on the pulse of their motivations and drivers – which naturally change – will help you to anticipate needs or wants and evolve your business.

TYPES OF MARKETS

Consumer

The Consumer Market includes those general consumers who buy products and services for personal use, or for use by family and friends. This is the market category you or I fall into when we're shopping for groceries or clothes, seeing a movie in the theatre, or going out for lunch. Retailers focus on this market category when marketing their goods or services.

Institutional

The Institutional Market serves society and provides products or services for the benefit of society. This includes hospitals, non-profit organizations, government organizations, schools and universities. Members of the Institutional Market purchase products to use in the provision of services to people in their care.

Business to Business (B2B)

The B2B Market is just what it seems to be: businesses that purchase the products and services of other businesses to run their operations. These purchases can include products that are used to manufacture other products (raw or technical), products that are needed for daily operations (such as office supplies), or services (such as accounting, shredding, and legal).

Reseller

This market can also be called the "Intermediary Market" because it consists of businesses that act as channels for goods and services between other markets. Goods are purchased and sold for a profit – without any alterations. Members of this market include wholesalers, retailers, resellers, and distributors.

DETERMINING YOUR TARGET MARKET

Product / Service Investigation

The process for determining your target market starts by examining exactly what your offering is, and what the average customer's motivation for purchasing it is. Start by answering the following questions:

Does your offering meet a basic need?	
Does your offering serve a particular want?	
Does your offering fulfill a desire?	
What is the lifecycle of your product / service?	

What is the availability of your offering?	
What is the cost of the average customer's purchase?	
What is the lifecycle of your offering?	
How many times or how often will customers purchase your offering?	
Do you foresee any upcoming changes in your industry or region that may affect the sale of your offering (positive/negative)?	

MARKET INVESTIGATION

♦ **On the ground.** Spend some time on the ground researching who your target market might be. If you're thinking about opening a coffee shop, hang out in the neighborhood at different times of the day to get a sense of the people who live, work, and play in the neighborhood. Notice their age, gender, clothing, and any other indications of income and activities.

♦ **At the competition.** Who is your direct competitor targeting? Is there a small niche that is being missed? Observing the clientele of your competition can help to build understanding of your target market, regardless of whether it is the same or opposite. For example, if you own a children's clothing boutique and the majority of middle-class mothers shop at the local department store, you may wish to focus on higher-income families as your target market.

+ **Online.** Many cities and towns – or at least regions – have demographic information available online. Research the ages, incomes, occupations, and other key pieces of information about the people who live in the area you operate your business. From this data, you will gain an understanding of the size of your total potential market.

+ **With existing customers.** Talk to your existing customers through focus groups or surveys. This is a great way to gather demographic and behavioral information, as well as genuine feedback about product or service quality and other information that will be useful in a business or marketing strategy.

WHO IS YOUR MARKET?

Based on your product / service and market investigations, you will be able to piece together a basic picture of your target market, and some of their general characteristics. Record some notes here. At this point, you may wish to be as specific as possible, or maintain some generalities. You can further segment your market in the next section.

CONSUMER TARGET MARKET FRAMEWORK

Market Type:	Consumer
Gender:	❏ Male ❏ Female
Age Range:	
Purchase Motivation:	❏ Meet a Need ❏ Serve a Want ❏ Fulfill a Desire
Activities:	
Income Range:	
Marital Status:	
Location:	❏ Neighborhood ❏ City ❏ Region ❏ Country
Other Notes:	

INSTITUTIONAL TARGET MARKET FRAMEWORK

Market Type:	Institutional	
Institution Type:	❑ Hospital ❑ School ❑ Charity ❑ Church	❑ Non-profit ❑ University ❑ Government
Purchase Motivation:	❑ Operational Need ❑ Client Want ❑ Client Desire	
Purpose of Institution:		
Institution's Client Base:		
Size:		
Location:	❑ Neighborhood ❑ Region	❑ City ❑ Country
Other Notes:		

B2B TARGET MARKET FRAMEWORK

Market Type:	Business to Business (B2B)
Company Size:	
Number of Employees:	
Purchase Motivation:	❑ Operations Need ❑ Strategy ❑ Functionality
Annual Revenue:	
Industry:	
Location(s):	
Purpose of Business:	
People, Culture & Values:	
Other Notes:	

RESELLER TARGET MARKET FRAMEWORK

Market Type:	Reseller
Industry:	
Client Base:	
Purchase Motivation:	❏ Operations Need ❏ Client Wants ❏ Functionality
Annual Revenue:	
Age:	
Location:	❏ Neighborhood ❏ City ❏ Region ❏ Country
Other Notes:	

YOUR TARGET MARKET: PUTTING IT TOGETHER

Based on the information you gather from your product / service and market investigations, you should have a clear vision of your realistic target market. Here are a few examples of how this information is put together and conclusions are drawn:

TARGET MARKET SAMPLE 1: CONSUMER MARKET

Business: Baby Clothing Boutique	**Business Purpose:** - Meet a need *(provide clothing for infants and children aged 0 to 5 years)* - Serve a want *(clothing is brand name only, and has a higher price point than the competition)*
Market Type: Consumer	
Gender: Women	
Marital Status: Married	
Market Observations: - located on Main Street of Anytown, a street that is seeing many new boutiques open up, proximate to the main shopping mall two blocks from popular mid-range restaurant that is busy at lunch	**Industry Predictions:** - large number of new housing developments in the city and surrounding areas - two new schools in construction - expect to see an influx of new families move to town from Anycity
Competition Observations: - baby clothing also available at two local department stores, and one second-hand shop on opposite side of town	**Online Research:** - half of Anytown's population is female, and 25% have children under the age of 15 years - Anytown's population is expected to increase by 32% within three years - The average household income for Anytown is $75,000 annually
TARGET MARKET: The target market can then be described as married mothers with children under five years old, between the ages of 25 and 45, who have recently moved to Anytown from Anycity, and have a household income of at least $100K annually.	

TARGET MARKET SAMPLE 2: B2B MARKET

Business: Confidential Paper Shredding	**Target Business Size:** Small to Medium
Market Type: B2B (Business to Business)	**Target Business Revenue:** $500K to $1M
Business Purpose: - Meet an operations need *(provide confidential on-site shredding services for business documents)*	**Target Business Type:** - produce or handle a variety of sensitive paper documentation - accountants, lawyers, real estate agents, etc.
Market Observations: - there are two main areas of office buildings and industrial warehouses in Anycity - three more office towers are being constructed, and will be completed this year	**Industry Predictions:** - the professional sector is seeing revenue growth of 24% over last year, which indicates increased client billing and staff recruitment
Competition Observations: - one confidential shredding company serves the region, covering Anycity and the surrounding towns - provide regular *(weekly or biweekly)* service, but does not have the capacity to handle large volumes at one time	**Online Research:** - Anycity's biggest employment sectors are: manufacturing, tourism, food services, and professional services
TARGET MARKET: The target market can then be described as small to medium sized businesses in the professional sector with an annual revenue of $500K to $1M who require both regular and infrequent large volume paper shredding services.	

SEGMENTING YOUR MARKET

Your market segments are the groups within your target market – broken down by a determinant in one of the following four categories:

- Demographics
- Psychographics
- Geographics
- Behaviors

Segmenting your target market into several more specific groups allows you to further tailor your marketing campaign and more specifically position your product or service. You may wish to divide your ad campaign into four sections, and target four specific markets with messages that will most resonate with the audience.

For example, the baby clothing store may choose to segment its target market by psychographics, or lifestyle. If the larger target market is *married females with children under five, between the ages of 25 and 45, who have a household income of at least $100K annually*, it can be broken down into the following lifestyle segments:

+ Fitness-oriented mothers

+ Career-oriented mothers

+ New mothers

With these three categories, unique marketing messages can be created that speak to the hot-buttons of each segment. The more accurate and specific you can make communications with your target market, the greater impact you will have on your revenues.

MARKET SEGMENTATION VARIABLES

Demographic	Psychographic	Geographic	Behavioristic
Age	Personality	Region	Brand Loyalty
Income	Lifestyle	Country	Product Usage
Gender	Values	City	Purchase
Generation	Attitude	Area	Frequency
Nationality	Motivation	Neighborhood	Profitability
Ethnicity	Activities	Density	Readiness to Buy
Marital Status	Interests	Climate	User Status
Family Size			
Occupation			
Religion			
Language			
Education			
Employment Type			
Housing Type			
Housing			
Ownership			
Political			
Affiliation			

UNDERSTANDING YOUR TARGET MARKET

Once you have determined who your market is, make a point of learning everything you can about them. You need to have a strong understanding of who they are, what they like, where they shop, why they buy, and how they spend their time. Remind yourself that you may think you know your market, but until you have verified the information, you'll be driving your marketing strategy blind.

Also be aware that markets change, just like people. Just because you knew your market when you started your business 10 years ago, doesn't mean you know it now. Regular market research is part of any successful business plan, and a great habit to start.

Types of Market Research

SURVEYS

The simplest way to gather information from your clients or target market is through a survey. You can craft a questionnaire full of questions about your product, service, market demographics, buyer motivations, and so on. Plus, anonymous surveys will produce the most accurate information since names are not attached to the results or specific comments.

Depending on the purpose—whether it is to gather demographic information, product or service feedback, or other data—there are a number of ways to administer a survey.

1. Telephone

Telephone surveys are a more time-consuming option, but have the benefit of live communication with your target market. Generally, it is best to have a third party conduct this type of survey to gather the most honest feedback. This is the method that market researchers use for polling, which is highly reliable.

2. Online

Online surveys are the easiest to administer yourself. There a many web-based services that quickly and easily allow to you custom create your survey, and send it to your email marketing list. These services can also analyze, summarize and interpret the results on your behalf. Keep in mind that the results include only those who are motivated to respond, which may slant your results.

3. Paper-based

Paper surveys are seldom used, and can prove to be an inefficient method. Like online surveys, your results are based on the feedback of those who were motivated for one reason or another to respond. However, the time and effort involved in taking the survey, filing it out, and returning it to your place of business may deter people from participating.

Keep in mind that surveys can be complex to administer, and consume more time and resources than you have planned. If you have the budget, consider hiring a professional market research firm to lead or assist with the process. This will also ensure that the methodology is standard practice, and will garner the most accurate results.

Website Analysis

Tracking your website traffic is an excellent way to research your existing and potential customer's interests and behavior. From this information, you can ensure the design, structure and content of your website is catering to the people who use it – and the people you want to use it.

User-friendly website traffic analytics programs can easily show you who is visiting your site, where they are from, and what pages of your site they are viewing. Services like Google Analytics can tell you what page they arrive at, where they click to, how much time they spend on each page, and on which page they leave the site.

This is powerful (and free!) information to have in your market research, and easy to monitor monthly or weekly, depending on the needs of your business.

Customer Purchase Data (Consumer Behavior)

If you do not have the budget to conduct your own professional market research, you can use existing resources on consumer behavior. While this data may not be specific to your region or city, general consumer research is actual data that can be helpful in confirming assumptions you may have made about your target market.

Your customer loyalty program or Point of Sale system may also be of help in tracking customer purchases and identifying trends in purchase behavior. If you can track who is buying, what they're buying and how often they're buying, you'll have an arsenal of powerful insight into your existing client base.

Focus Groups

Focus groups look at the psychographic and behavioristic aspects of your target market. Groups of six to 12 people are gathered and asked general and specific questions about their purchase motivations and behaviors. These questions could relate to your business in particular, or to the general industry.

Focus group sessions can also be time consuming to organize and facilitate, so consider hiring the services of a professional market research firm. You may also receive more honest information if a third party is asking the questions, and receiving the responses from focus group participants.

For cost savings, consider partnering with an associate in the same industry who is not a direct competitor, and who would benefit from the same market data.

Generating an Unlimit- ed Amount of Leads for Your Business

✦ ✦ ✦

Where do your customers come from?

Most people would probably choose advertising as an answer. Or referrals. Or direct mail campaigns. This may seem true, but it's not really accurate.

Your customers come from leads that have been turned into sales. Each customer goes through a two-step process before they arrive with their wallets open. They have been converted from a member of a target market, to a lead, then to a customer.

So, would it not stand to reason then, that when you advertise or send any marketing material out to your target market, that you're not really trying to generate customers? That instead, you're trying to generate leads.

When you look at your marketing campaign from this perspective, the idea of generating leads as compared to customers seems a lot less daunting. The pressure of closing sales is no longer placed on advertisements or brochures.

From this perspective, **the general purpose of your advertising and marketing efforts is then to generate leads from qualified customers.** Seems easy enough, doesn't it?

WHERE ARE YOUR LEADS COMING FROM?

If I asked you to tell me the top three ways you generate new sales leads, what would you say?

- ✦ Advertising?
- ✦ Word of mouth?
- ✦ Networking?
- ✦ ...don't know?

The first step toward increasing your leads is in understanding how many leads you currently get on a regular basis, as well as where they come from. Otherwise, how will you know when you're getting more phone calls or walk-in customers?

If you don't know where your leads come from, start today. Start asking every customer that comes through your door, "how did you hear about us?" or "what brought you in today?" Ask every customer that calls where they found your telephone number, or email address. Then, record the information for at least an entire week.

When you're finished, take a look at your spreadsheet and write your top three lead generators here:

1. _____

2. _____

3. _____

FROM LEAD TO CUSTOMER: CONVERSION RATES

Leads mean nothing to your business unless you convert them into customers. You could get hundreds of leads from a single advertisement, but unless those leads result in purchases, it's been a largely unsuccessful (and costly) campaign.

The ratio of leads (potential customers) to transactions (actual customers) is called your conversion rate. Simply divide the number of customers who actually purchased something by the number of customers who inquired about your product or service, and multiply by 100.

 # transactions / # leads x 100 = % conversion rate

If, in a given week, I have 879 customers come into my store, and 143 of them purchase something, the formula would look like this:

[143 (customers) / 879 (leads)] x 100 = 16.25% conversion rate

What's Your Conversion Rate?

Based on the formula above, you can see that the higher your conversion rate, the more profitable the business.

Your next step is to determine your own current conversion rate. Add up the number of leads you sourced in the last section, and divide that number into the total transactions that took place in the same week.

Write your conversion rate here:

_____

QUALITY (OR QUALIFIED) LEADS

Based on our review of conversion rates, we can see that the number of leads you generate means nothing unless those leads are being converted into customers.

So what affects your ability (and the ability of your team) to turn leads into customers? Do you need to improve your scripts? Your product or service? Find a more competitive edge in the marketplace?

Maybe. But the first step toward increasing conversion rates is to evaluate the leads you are currently generating, and make sure those leads are the right ones.

What are Quality Leads?

Potential customers are potential customers, right? Anyone who walks into your store or picks up the phone to call your business could be convinced to purchase from you, right? Not necessarily, but this is a common assumption most business owners make.

Quality leads are the people who are the most likely to buy your product or service. They are the qualified buyers who comprise your target market. Anyone might walk in off the street to browse a furniture store – regardless of whether or not they are in the market for a new couch or bed frame. This lead is solely interested in browsing, and is not likely to be converted to a customer.

A quality lead would be someone looking for a new kitchen table, and who specifically drove to that same furniture store because a friend had raved about the service they received that month. **These are the kinds of leads you need to focus on generating.**

How Do You Get Quality Leads?

+ **Know your target market.** Get a handle on who your customers are – the people who are most likely to buy your product or service. Know their age, sex, income, and purchase motivations. From that information you can determine how best to reach your specific audience.

+ **Focus on the 80/20 rule.** A common statistic in business is that 80% of your revenue comes from 20% of your customers (this percentage may fluctuate depending on your business type). These are your star clients, or your ideal clients. These are the clients you should focus your efforts on recruiting. This is the easiest way to grow your business and your income.

+ **Get specific.** Focus not only on who you want to attract, but how you're going to attract them. If you're trying to generate leads from a specific market segment, craft a unique offer to get their attention.

+ **Be proactive.** Once you've generated a slew of leads, make sure you have the resources to follow up on them. Be diligent and aggressive, and follow up in a timely manner. You've done the work to get them, now reel them in.

GET MORE LEADS FROM YOUR EXISTING STRATEGIES

Increasing your lead generation doesn't necessarily mean diving in and implementing an expensive array of new marketing strategies. Marketing and customer outreach for the purpose of lead generation can be inexpensive, and bring a high return on investment.

You are likely already implementing many of these strategies. With a little tweaking or refinement, you can easily double your leads, and ensure they are more qualified.

Here are some popular ways to generate quality leads:

Direct Mail to Your Ideal Customers

Direct mail is one of the fastest and most effective ways to generate leads that will build your business. It's a simple strategy – in fact, you're probably already reaching out to potential clients through direct mail letters with enticing offers.

The secret to doubling your results is to craft your direct mail campaigns specifically for a highly targeted audience of your *ideal* customers.

Your ideal customers are the people who will buy the most of your products or services. They are the customers who will buy from you over and over again, and refer your business to their friends. They are the group of 20% of your clients who make up 80% of your revenue.

Identify your ideal customers

Who are your ideal customers? What is their age, sex, income, location and purchase motivation? Where do they live? How do they spend their money? Be as specific as possible.

Once you have identified who your ideal customers are, you can begin to determine how you can go about reaching them. Will you mail to households or apartment buildings? Families or retirees? Direct mail lists are available for purchase from a wide range of companies, and can be segregated into a variety of demographic and socio-graphic categories.

Craft a special offer

Create an offer that's too good to refuse – not for your entire target market, but for your ideal customer. How can you cater to their unique needs and wants? What will be irresistible for them?

For example, if you operate a furniture store, your target market is a broad range of people. However, if you are targeting young families, your offer will be much different than one you may craft for empty-nesters.

Court them for their business

Don't stop at a single mail-out. Sometimes people will throw your letter away two or three times before they are motivated to act. Treat your direct mail campaign like a courtship, and understand that it will happen over time.

First send a letter introducing yourself, and your irresistible offer. Then follow up on a monthly basis with additional letters, newsletters, offers, or flyers. Repetition and reinforcement of your presence is how your customer will go from saying, "who is this company" to "I buy from this company."

Advertise for lead generation

Statistics show that nearly 50% of all purchase decisions are motivated by advertising. It can also be a relatively cost effective way of generating leads.

We've already discussed the importance of ensuring your advertisements are purpose-focused. The general purpose of most advertisements is to increase sales – which starts with leads. However ads that are created solely for lead generation – that is, to get the customers to pick up the phone or walk in the store – are a category of their own.

Lead generation ads are simply designed and create a sense of curiosity or mystery. Often, they feature an almost unbelievable offer. Their purpose is not to convince the customer to buy, but to contact the business for more information.

As always, when you are targeting your ideal audience, you'll need to ensure that your ads are placed prominently in publications that your audience reads. This doesn't mean you have to fork over the cash for expensive display ads. Inexpensive advertising in e-mail newsletters, classifieds, and the yellow pages are very effective for lead generation.

Here are some tips for lead generation advertising:

Leverage low-cost advertising

Place ads in the yellow pages, classifieds section, e-mail newsletters, and online. If your target audience is technology savvy, consider new forms of advertising like Facebook and Google Adwords.

Spark curiosity

Don't give them all the information they need to make a decision. Ask them to contact you for the full story, or the complete details of the seemingly outrageous offer.

Grab them with a killer headline

Like all advertising, a compelling headline is essential. Focus on the greatest benefits to the customer, or feature an unbelievable offer.

Referrals and host beneficiary relationships

A referral system is one of the most profitable systems you can create in your business. The beauty is once it's set up, it often runs itself.

Customers that come to you through referrals are often your "ideal customers." They are already trusting and willing to buy. This is one of the most cost-effective methods of generating new business, and is often the most profitable. These referral clients will buy more, faster, and refer further business to your company.

Referrals naturally happen without much effort for reputable businesses, but with a proactive referral strategy you'll certainly double or triple your referrals. Sometimes, you just need to ask!

Here are some easy strategies you can begin to implement today:

Referral incentives

Give your customers a reason to refer business to you. Reward them with discounts, gifts, or free service in exchange for a successful referral.

Referral program

Offer new customers a free product or service to get them in the door. Then, at the end of the transaction, give them three more 'coupons' for the same free product or service that they can give to their friends. Do the same with their friends. This ongoing program will bring you more business than you can imagine.

Host-beneficiary relationships

Forge alliances with non-competitive companies who target your ideal customers. Create cross-promotion and cross-referral direct mail campaigns that benefit both businesses.

LEAD MANAGEMENT SYSTEMS

Once your lead generation strategies are in place, you'll also need a system to manage incoming inquiries. You'll need to ensure you receive enough information from each lead to follow up on at a later date. You'll also need to create a system to organize that information, and track the lead as it is converted into a sale.

Gathering Information from Your Leads

Here is a list of information you should gather from your leads. This list can be customized to the needs of your business, and the type of information you can realistically ask for from your potential customers.

- ✦ Company Name
- ✦ Name of Contact
- ✦ Alternate Contact Person
- ✦ Mailing Address

- Phone Number
- Fax Number
- Cell Phone
- Email Address
- Website Address
- Product of Interest
- Other Competitors Engaged

Lead List Management Methods:

Once you have gathered information from your lead, you'll need a system to organize their information and keep a detailed contact history.

The simplest way to do this is with a database program, but you can also use a variety of hard copy methods.

Electronic Database Programs

- High level of organization available
- Unlimited space for notes and record-keeping
- Data-entry required
- Examples include: MS Outlook, MS Excel, Maximizer
- Customer Relationship Management Software

Index Cards

- Variety of sizes: 3x5, 4X6 or 5X8
- Basic contact information on one side
- Notes on the other side
- Easy to organize and sort

Rolodex System

- Maintain more contacts than index card system
- Easily organized and compact
- Basic contact information on one side

+ Notes on the other side

+ Can keep phone conversation and purchase details

Notebook

+ Best if leads are managed by a single person

+ Lots of room for notes

+ Inexpensive

+ Difficult to re-organize

+ Best for smaller lists

Business Card Organizer

+ Best for small lists – under 100

+ Limited space for notes

+ No data entry required

+ Rolodex-style, or clear binder pages

Copywriting for Profits

✦ ✦ ✦

When it comes to marketing, we all know that what you say is just as important as how you say it.

In fact, I would argue that how you say something is even more important than what you have to say.

Think about it. The whole purpose of communicating is to get a message to its intended audience. In business, this means telling your target market why they should buy your product or service, and why they should buy it from you.

You could have the best, most irresistible offer out there, but if you can't get your audience to pay attention to your ad, it's worthless. You may offer the solution to their biggest frustration, but if you can't get them to read beyond your headline, it means nothing.

Effective copywriting gets your message to your target audience and then leads them to act. **Effective copywriting gets you the sale.**

GOOD COPY, BAD COPY

There are a number of misconceptions out there when it comes to copywriting for marketing collateral.

The first is that good copy must be clever (or witty, funny, dramatic, ironic, etc.). People get wrapped up in the idea that their ads need to compete with the ads on the pages of Vanity Fair – or the New York Times. They feel that their campaign needs to be littered with clever words that allude to the pop culture of the day, or position their company as "hip" or sophisticated.

This, in my experience, is rubbish.

The second assumption most business owners make is that good copy is the backbone of a successful ad or marketing campaign. I can't tell you how many good copywriters I've seen take the blame for a bad offer, or poorly positioned product.

The third misconception is that you need to be a good writer to write good copy. Or, if you're not a good writer, that you need to spend thousands of dollars on a copywriter for each of your marketing pieces.

That's rubbish, too.

So, then, what is good copy? And how do you write it?

THE PURPOSE OF YOUR COPY

Here are the key points you need to remember when crafting your advertisements:

+ A good headline *gets your readers to read the first sentence.*

+ A good first sentence *gets your readers to read the second sentence.*

+ And so on and on until the end of your marketing piece; or, the close of the sale.

Simple, isn't it?

The copy in your marketing materials is intended to persuade your audience to buy what you have to offer – one sentence at a time. Once you understand that copywriting is persuasive writing, not creative or technical writing, you will have much more success with your copywriting efforts.

Persuasive copy can be written in a number of ways – which we will discuss later in the section – but always includes:

+ a compelling, shocking, or gripping headline

+ a strong promise

+ a heavy focus on benefits, not features

+ proof to back up your claims

Compelling writing slowly builds a case, and leads the reader down a specific path to the final destination: the sale. The argument or message is built up over several sentences, or paragraphs, until the reader is primed and ready for the question.

For example, if you came right out in your headline and said, "Buy Tommy's Sprockets to Solve Your Problems", your highly skeptical audience would not give your ad a second glance. You've asked for the sale right up front, before building some trust and slowly persuading your readers.

However, if you took the time to build your case, the ad would read something like this:

DON'T BUY ANOTHER SPROCKET UNTIL YOU READ THIS

Did you know that the average sprocket is made with only 25% authentic materials? To speed up production and reduce costs, sprocket manufacturing over the last decade has begun to rely heavily on artificial materials.

Would you trust the safety of your family to a product that reduces quality to preserve profit?

At Tommy's Sprockets, we put the safety of your family first. Our sprockets are stronger and safer, because we still make them the old fashioned way – with 100% authentic materials and a lifetime guarantee.

Sure, they cost a little more than the average sprocket, but how much more would you pay for the safety of your family?

This ad isn't going to win any Pulitzer Prizes, but it doesn't need to. It engages the audience, communicates benefits, supports with features, and paints a compelling argument.

HEADLINES

Headlines are so crucial to the copywriting in your advertisement or sales letter that they deserve an entire section in this chapter.

Your headline is the first chance you have to make an impression on your target audience. Quite possibly, it is also your only chance. Without a headline that grabs your reader by the neck and focuses on what you have to say, the remainder of your ad is useless.

That's why even the greatest copywriters spend 50% of their time on the headline, and 50% on the rest of the copy.

With that in mind, it's important to note that your headline needs to do more than simply grab the attention of your potential readers. It also needs to tell them why they should care – your headline needs to send a full message that informs and encourages them to read onwards.

The most effective way to do this is to make an offer or promise to the reader that makes the time they invest in reading your ad worthwhile.

Seems like a lot for 8 to 10 words, doesn't it?

Headline Length

The general understanding when it comes to headline length is the shorter the better. But this comes from headline creation for newspapers and magazines, where space is crunched and nothing is up for sale.

In fact, based on studies done in the direct mail industry, 40% to 50% of the most effective headlines are more than eight words in length – meaning there are really no hard and fast rules for headline length.

Another marketing example of headline length is in sales letters. I'm sure you've seen headlines in sales letters that actually comprise small paragraphs. This is the opposite way of thinking from newspaper headlines, but in this medium it works.

The point is, if you need more than eight words to get your message across, then use more.

Headline Readers: The 80/20 Rule

According to readership statistics, eight out of 10 people read headlines, but only two of 10 will read the rest of the advertisement or letter. This proves the importance of crafting powerful, meaningful headlines. It also proves that an effective headline is the golden key to getting the rest of the piece read.

So, it would stand to reason that the better your headline, the better the chances of improving the number of people who will read the rest of your advertisement or sales letter.

Headline Types

Direct Headlines simply state the offer or proposition in as clear a manner as possible. *All winter clothing 30% off.*

News Headlines typically announce a new product or piece of information and mimic a headline you would read in a newspaper. *Jonny launches new line of improved sprockets.*

The Question Headline asks a question that the reader can relate to or would be compelled to read on to find the answer. *Do you want clearer skin?*

The 'How to' Headline tells the reader the body copy or product will explain step by step instructions for something of interest to the reader. *How to save $1,000 in energy costs this year.*

Command Headline is one of the strongest headline types, and commands the reader to do something. *Make your dreams come true today.*

The '7 Reasons Why' Headline tells the reader the body copy will include 7 (or another number less than seven) points that will either back up a claim or illustrate product benefits. *7 reasons why your teenagers won't listen to you.*

Testimonial Headlines leverages the power of outsider and expert opinion and quotes them directly in the headline. *"Tommy's sprockets have changed my life" says Brad Pitt.*

In summary, your headline should:

+ Be immediately engaging

+ Be useful and relevant to the reader

+ Convey information

+ Trigger an emotional reaction

+ Include an offer

+ Intrigue your audience

STRATEGIES FOR BETTER COPYWRITING

Simplify, Simplify, Simplify

Good copy is written in clear, simple language with short sentence structure. It's conversational and reads like you are speaking to a friend or colleague.

Important points – like benefits – are listed in numbered or bullet format and traditional grammar is sacrificed for brevity.

Always read your copy before you finalize it and take out any unnecessary words. Find the shortest way to communicate the most information.

Be More Persuasive

Persuasion is an important technique for structuring your copy. While there is no clear formula for any type of copywriting, persuasive copy consistently includes the following elements:

- Has a reader focus from the very beginning

- Each paragraph or section supports the main argument

- Is highly specific and provides proof to support claims

- Includes credible proof like statistics and expert opinion

- Returns the focus to the reader as often as possible

Persuasive writing convinces the reader that they should believe what you say and do you what you say, and that there is something in it for them if they do. Again, there is no formula for this and no clear content rules, but there are some strategies you can use to make your writing more persuasive.

Repeat your point over and over

Repetition is a powerful and essential tool when crafting persuasive copy. It often will take several attempts at communicating before someone truly understands what you're saying. The benefit is that the more you say it, and the more ways you say it, the more likely your audience will believe it.

Of course, don't literally repeat yourself verbatim in your copy. Use a few different techniques to communicate the same point – for example, state it directly, tell a story, then repeat it again in your summary.

Give them reasons why

Backup your claims and requests with good reasons and leverage the power of the word 'because.' Studies have proven that even if the reason doesn't make any sense, or isn't directly related to the claim, people will be more likely to believe you simply based on the fact you backed up what you had to say.

Make comparisons to prove a point

Use the power of metaphors, analogies, and similes in your writing. This gives you an opportunity to relate the point you are trying to make directly to something the reader can relate to and understands to be true.

This is effective for making comparisons between like subjects, as well as unlike subjects, depending on the point you are trying to make.

Answer silent objections

Show that you understand the reader's point of view and thought process by answering questions you know they will be considering in their minds.

While you will not be able to address all potential objections in a single piece, or think of all potential objections your reader may raise, you can definitely dispute the most common arguments against what you are claiming.

Tell a story

Storytelling is an effective technique to use in all aspects of your copywriting. People relate to the experiences of others, and strive to learn from or compare themselves to the characters in the anecdotes. The story ends up doing the persuading for you.

Focus on Benefits

This is an obvious aspect of your messaging that you will feature in every piece you write, but it's not always easy to do well. Many writers end up featuring a slew of fake benefits instead of real ones.

Real benefits are things the reader actually cares about. For example, if you sold cough syrup you would want to explain how it eases the cold or flu symptoms, and not that it cures the illness. The symptoms are what are bothering the reader – that's what aspect of the product they care about and will make their purchase based on.

Make a Better Offer

Compel the reader to act with a stronger offer – one that they just can't possibly refuse. Make one that seems just believable enough to take action and reap the rewards.

A strong offer features a product or service with a high perceived value for a low cost. It could be a package of products offered for a lower price than the sum of the individual products, or a "free gift" with purchase.

Use Words that Work

Another misconception when it comes to copywriting is that it needs to be 100% unique. I'm not saying you should blatantly plagiarize other writer's work, but you should definitely pay attention to what works.

This includes how an ad is structured, how a point is made, or the hierarchy of the content. It also includes word choice. Certain words in marketing have been proven to have a stronger impact on general consumers than others.

There are tools that are easily available to you that will provide a list or database of effective words for use in advertising. Research online or invest in a software programs like Glyphus to use as a resource. Or become a member of my Income Generation Academy and get a list of powerful words, elevator pitches, access to our $1 million marketing library and dozens of tactics and strategies to market your business.

Offer a Guarantee

A guarantee is another technique that will compel a potential customer to take action. A strong guarantee takes the risk involved in purchase decisions away from the customer, and puts it on the seller.

Tell your customer that if your product or service doesn't deliver the performance or results you have promised, you'll give them their money back or compensate them in a way that will make it right.

Creating a
Powerful Offer

✦ ✦ ✦

I'm not going to beat around the bush on this one:

Your offer is the granite foundation of your marketing campaign.

Get it right, and everything else will fall into place. Your headline will grab readers, your copy will sing, your ad layout will hardly matter, and you will have customers running to your door.

Get it wrong, and even the best looking, best-written campaign will sink like the Titanic.

A powerful offer is an irresistible offer. It's an offer that gets your audience frothing at the mouth and clamoring over each other all the way to your door. An offer that makes your readers pick up the phone and open their wallets.

Irresistible offers make your potential customers think, "I'd be crazy not to take him up on that," or "An offer like this doesn't come around very often." They instill a sense of emotion, of desire, and ultimately, urgency.

Make it easy for customers to purchase from you the first time, and spend your time keeping them coming back.

I'll say it again: **get it right, and everything else will fall into place.**

THE CRUX OF YOUR MARKETING CAMPAIGN

As you work your way through this program, you will find that nearly every chapter discusses the importance of a powerful offer as related to your marketing strategy or promotional campaign.

There's a reason for this. The powerful offer is more often than not the reason a customer will open their wallets. It is how you generate leads, and then convert them into loyal customers. The more dramatic, unbelievable, and valuable the offer is the more dramatic and unbelievable the response will be.

Many companies spend thousands of dollars on impressive marketing campaigns in glossy magazines and big city newspapers. They send massive direct mail campaigns on a regular basis; yet don't receive an impressive or massive response rate.

These companies do not yet understand that simply providing information on their company and the benefits of their product is not enough to get customers to act. There is no reason to pick up the phone or visit the store, right now.

Your powerful, irresistible offer can:

+ Increase leads

+ Drive traffic to your website or business

+ Move old product

+ Convert leads into customers

+ Build your customer database

WHAT MAKES A POWERFUL OFFER?

A powerful offer is one that makes the most people respond, and take action. It gets people running to spend money on your product or service.

Powerful offers nearly always have an element of urgency and of scarcity. They give your audience a reason to act immediately, instead of put it off until a later date.

Urgency relates to time. The offer is only available until a certain date, during a certain period of the day, or if you act within a few hours of seeing the ad. The customer needs to act now to take advantage of the offer.

Scarcity relates to quantity. There are only a certain number of customers who will be able to take advantage of the offer. There may be a limited number of spaces, a limited number of products, or simply a limited number of people the business will provide the offer to. Again, this requires that the customer acts immediately to reap the high value for low cost.

Powerful offers also:

Offer great value. Customers perceive the offer as having great value – more than a single product on its own, or the product at its regular price. It is clear that the offer takes the reader's needs and wants into consideration.

Make sense to the reader. They are simple and easy to understand if read quickly. Avoid percentages – use half off or 2 for 1 instead of 50% off. There are no "catches" or requirements; no fine print.

Seem logical. The offer doesn't come out of thin air. There is a logical reason behind it – a holiday, end of season, anniversary celebration, or new product. People can get suspicious of offers that seem "too good to be true" and have no apparent purpose.

Provide a premium. The offer provides something extra to the customer, like a free gift, or free product or service. They feel they are getting something extra for no extra cost. Premiums are perceived to have more value than discounts.

Remember that when your target market reads your offer, they will be asking the following questions:

1. What are you offering me?

2. What's in it for me?

3. What makes me sure I can believe you?

4. How much do I have to pay for it?

THE MOST POWERFUL TYPES OF OFFERS

Decide what kind of offer will most effectively achieve your objectives. Are you trying to generate leads, convert customers, build a database, move old product off the shelves, or increase sales?

Consider what type of offer will be of most value to your ideal customers – what offer will make them act quickly.

Free Offer

This type of offer asks customers to act immediately in exchange for something free. This is a good strategy to use to build a customer database or mailing list. Offer a free consultation, free consumer report, or other item of low cost to you but of high perceived value.

You can also advertise the value of the item you are offering for free. For example, act now and you'll receive a free consultation, worth $75 dollars. This will dramatically increase your lead generation, and allow you to focus on conversion when the customer comes through the door or picks up the phone.

The Value Added Offer

Add additional services or products that cost you very little, and combine them with other items to increase their attractiveness. This increases the perception of value in the customer's mind, which will justify increasing the price of a product or service without incurring extra hard costs to your business.

Package Offer

Package your products or services together in a logical way to increase the perceived value as a whole. Discount the value of the package by a small margin, and position it as a "start-up kit" or "special package." By packaging goods of mixed values, you will be able to close more high-value sales. For example: including a free desk-jet printer with every computer purchase.

Premium Offer

Offer a bonus product or service with the purchase of another. This strategy will serve your bottom line much better than discounting. This includes 2 for 1 offers, offers that include free gifts, and in-store credit with purchases over a specific dollar amount.

Urgency Offer

As I mentioned above, offers that include an element of urgency enjoy a better response rate, as there is a reason for your customers to act immediately. Give the offer a deadline or limit the number of spots available.

Guarantee Offer

Offer to take the risk of making a purchase away from your customers. Guarantee the performance or results of your product or service, and offer to compensate the customer with their money back if they are not satisfied. This will help overcome any fear or reservations about your product, and make it more likely for your leads to become customers.

CREATE YOUR POWERFUL OFFER

1. Pick a single product or service.

Focus on only one product or service – or one product or service type – at a time. This will keep your offer clear, simple, and easy to understand. This can be an area of your business you wish to grow, or old product that you need to move off the shelves.

2. Decide what you want your customers to do.

What are you looking to achieve from your offer? If it is to generate more leads, then you'll need your customer to contact you. If it is to quickly sell old product, you'll need your customer to come into the store and buy it. Do you want them to visit your website? Sign up for your newsletter? How long do they have to act? Be clear about your call to action, and state it clearly in your offer.

3. Dream up the biggest, best offer.

First, think of the biggest, best things you could offer your customers – regardless of cost and ability. Don't limit yourself to a single type of offer, combine several types of offers to increase value. Offer a premium, plus a guarantee, with a package offer. Then take a look at what you've created, and make the necessary changes so it is realistic.

4. Run the numbers.

Finally, make sure the offer will leave you with some profit – or at least allows you to break even. You don't want to publish an outrageous offer that will generate a tremendous number of leads, but leave you broke. Remember that each customer has an acquisition cost, as well as a lifetime value. The amount of their first purchase may allow you to break even, but the amount of their subsequent purchases may make you a lovely profit.

Risk Reversal to Increase Sales

✦ ✦ ✦

What is the biggest objection you need to overcome when closing a sale? Is it cost? Belief in what you have to say? Confidence in your product or service?

While it is a different answer for every business, every business has to deal with some element of customer fear or hesitation before a monetary transaction.

The reality is that even if you overcome these objections and close the sale, your customer walks away carrying 99% of the risk associated with the purchase. If the product doesn't work, breaks down, or doesn't perform to expectations, your customer has parted with their dollars in exchange for disappointment.

In marketing, your objective is to generate as many leads as possible, then to convert each lead into a customer, or sale. The ratio of leads to closed sales is called your conversion rate.

What if you could eliminate the risk involved in a transaction? Would you turn more leads into customers? The answer is absolutely.

Introducing a risk reversal element into your marketing message or unique offer is a powerful way to give yourself an edge on the competition and close more sales. But how exactly are you going to do this?

It's easy – just give them a guarantee.

THE POWER OF GUARANTEES

What is Risk Reversal?

Risk reversal simply refers to reversing the risk associated with a transaction – transferring it from the customer to the vendor.

Everyone can think of a handful of times they have purchased a product or service that did not deliver on their expectations. A time where a salesperson made them a promise and did not deliver. A time where they lost money on a faulty product or bogus service.

Fear of being burned or taken advantage of prevents many people from spending their money. Customers can also be very wary of buying a product or service for the first time.

Providing a strong guarantee eliminates the majority of risk involved in the purchase, and breaks down natural barriers in the sales process. Guarantees will often shorten the sales process all together – skipping any discussion of objections – because the customer does not see any risk in "trying the product out."

There is also a growing consumer expectation when it comes to guarantees. Many stores will take back anything the customer has not been happy with, and return money or store credit. Popular health food stores encourage customers to try new or unfamiliar products by promising a hassle-free, no questions asked return process. A guarantee or easy return policy can be the difference between choosing one business over its competition.

Your customers buy results, not products or services

The strongest guarantee you can make is on results, not products or services.

If you guarantee that your customer will receive the benefits or results they are looking for, the specific product or service they'll need to achieve those results becomes irrelevant.

People buy benefits and results. For example, they don't buy water purifiers; they buy the benefit of enjoying clean, fresh-tasting water. They don't buy lawn sprinkler systems; they buy a healthy green lawn.

Once you understand what specific benefit or solution your customers are seeking, find a way to guarantee they'll receive or experience that solution. If they don't, you'll compensate them for it.

Remember what you have guaranteed

While guarantees will increase sales for most businesses, they can also be the fast track to business failure if their product or service isn't a quality one. Take the time to ensure you have a strong offering before you implement a guarantee.

Guarantees are most effective when you are selling someone something they need or want – not when you are trying to convince someone to purchase something they have no use for.

INCREASING CONVERSION RATES WITH A GUARANTEE

Guarantees can help your business turn more qualified leads into repeat customers. Strong guarantees are big and bold, but also realistic. They're just a little bit better than your competition, but consistent with the industry's standards.

Your conversion rate

As stated previously, your conversion rate is the percentage of clients you convert from leads into customers. The higher your conversion rate, the more revenue you will generate.

Guarantees encourage and increase conversion. They motivate potential customers to buy – and to buy from you – because you stand behind what you sell in a big way. There is no risk involved in purchasing what you have to offer.

Creating your guarantee

So you're convinced your business – and your customers – would benefit from a strong guarantee. Now what? What are you going to guarantee? How are you going to position it?

Once again, this goes back to your target audience and your product or service. What are some of the major objections your potential customers raise during the sales process? What kind of risk do they take on when they make a purchase? How much time will they need to test or experience your product or service?

Brainstorm a list of things about your industry that really frustrate your customers. They could be service-based (contractors that don't show up, employees who don't perform) or product-based (products that break, do not perform). Then, take a look at your list and decide how you can make sure these things do not happen. Think big – you can do a lot more than you think – then determine if you can actually make good on your promise. If you can't guarantee the first frustration, then move on to the second.

Here are some tips on writing your guarantee:

+ **Be specific.** Explain exactly what you are guaranteeing. Don't make vague guarantees that a product will "work" or a service will make you "happy". These words mean different things to different people. Guarantee specific performance or results.

+ **Include a clear timeframe.** Put a realistic timeframe on your guarantee. Very few products or services are good forever. Offer a 30-day or 90-day free trial; guarantee results within a set number of days or weeks. This can protect your company, and sets out clear expectations for your clients.

+ **Be bold.** Unbelievable guarantees get a customer's attention, so go as far as you realistically can with your claim. Find a way to stand out over the competition – which may also have a guarantee.

+ **Tell them what you'll do.** Explain what you'll do – how you'll compensate them – if your product or service doesn't deliver. Be specific, talk money, and go above and beyond.

IMPLEMENTING GUARANTEES

Tell your clients!

Put your guarantee everywhere – your website, brochures, receipt tape, in-store signage, advertisements, and other promotional materials. It will only help attract customers if they know about it.

Send a newsletter to your existing client base informing them of your new guarantees – you never know how many customers you can convince to come back and spend more in your business.

Train your Staff

Once you have decided to offer your clients a guarantee, you need to ensure your staff are properly trained on the specific policies and procedures associated with that guarantee. If you offer different guarantees for different products and services, ensure this is made clear as well.

Presumably, your staff will be communicating the details of your guarantee, and fielding customer questions. They will have to know how to sell the product using the guarantee as a benefit, and understand every application of the guarantee in your business. Every scenario a customer may need to use it.

To ensure your staff is not making any false claims or promises, create a guarantee script for them to use and stick to. This will prevent customers from returning with false hopes for their money back, or other compensation.

RETURNS + CLAIMS

So, by now you must be thinking, "Great, I can convert more customers with a strong guarantee, and increase my sales. But what about the added risk I have taken on from my customers? Won't I start to see a ton of returns and service claims?" This is a valid question. Making a strong guarantee means standing by it and delivering on your promise. Inevitably, when you guarantee something, someone is going to take you up on that guarantee and make a claim. I'm going to answer this question in two parts:

1. **Stand behind your product or service.**

   You're not in business to scam customers. If you sell a product or service, and you believe in it enough to offer it to your customers, it is likely a quality product or genuine service.

   If this is a concern to you, consider implementing strong quality controls or stronger criteria for your merchandising. Companies that offer products and services that deliver results can offer the strongest guarantees.

   Of course you will get returns. You will have customers come in to take advantage of you. Just remember that as long as the increase in sales outweighs the claims, your guarantee strategy has been successful.

2. **Understand your customer's likely behavior.**

   The truth is that most customers will never take advantage of your guarantee – regardless of their satisfaction level. There are a number of reasons for this.

   The first is that most people can't be bothered to drive, mail, or otherwise seek a refund on an item under $50. Many let the timeframe slip by, and have an "oh well" attitude.

   The second is that most people don't like confrontation. There is usually an element of confrontation involved in telling someone you didn't like a product or service, and many people do not have the confidence to do so. They'd rather eat the cost than go through the process of asking for a refund.

Handling claims and returns:

If you do have your product returned, it is in your company's best interest to create a system for handling these customer interactions.

Create a claim form

Ensure that each customer who makes a claim about your product or service fills out a standard form. Doing so will help you prevent fraud, gather important information about the customer and their reasoning, and create a "hoop" for the customer to jump through if they want their money back.

Name	*Contact Information*
Date	*Salesperson*
Product	*Reason for claim*
Comments	*Follow-up*

Keep a claim or return log

Create a log or filing system for your claims. This will give you a snapshot of your guarantee program, a record-keeping system, and a wealth of information about each customer's experience and motivations.

Use the information

Take the claim forms your customers have filled out, and review them regularly. While some of the claims won't be genuine, there will be some real feedback you can use to improve your product or service, or to modify your guarantee. You may need to make it more realistic, or change the specifics.

Profit from Internet Marketing

✦ ✦ ✦

Is your business online? If not, it should be.

The internet is today's primary consumer research tool. If your business does not have an online presence, it is harder for customers to find and choose your business over the competition. With over 73% of North Americans online, it is no wonder that individuals and businesses in all industries are looking to the internet to enhance their marketing strategies.

Luckily, it has never been easier to establish and maintain a comprehensive online presence. Internet marketing, also referred to as online marketing, online advertising or e-marketing, is the fastest growing medium for marketing.

But it is not just company websites that users are viewing. Blogs, consumer reviews, chat rooms and a variety of social media are growing rapidly in popularity.

The internet is a very powerful tool for businesses if used strategically and effectively. It can be a cost saving alternative to traditional marketing approaches, and may be the most effective way to communicate with your target consumer.

A major advantage of the internet is that you are always open. Users can access your business 24 hours a day, 7 days a week, and depending on your business and the purpose of the website, visitors can also purchase goods at any time.

INTERNET MARKETING FOR EVERYONE

The internet is a great way to create product and brand awareness, develop relationships with consumers and share and exchange information. You can't afford not be taking advantage of online marketing opportunities because your competition is likely already there.

Internet marketing can take on many different forms. By creating and maintaining a website for your business, you are reaching out to a new consumer base. You can have full control over the messaging that users are receiving and have a global reach.

Internet marketing can be very cost effective. If you have a strong email database of your customers, an e-newsletter may be cheaper and more effective than post mail. You can deliver time sensitive materials immediately and can update your subscribers instantaneously.

Top 10 Websites (Globally)

1. Google.com
2. Facebook
3. You Tube
4. Yahoo.com
5. Baidu.com
6. Wikipedia.org
7. Twitter
8. Amazon
9. Linkedin
10. Qg.com

You will notice that half of these websites are search engines. An increasing number of consumers are first researching products, services and companies online, whether it be to compare products, complete a sale, or look for a future employer. Most people in the 18-35 age group obtain all of their information online—including news, weather, product research, etc. The remaining sites are interactive sites where users can upload information for social networking, or information sharing.

INTERNET MARKETING STRATEGIES

Internet marketing – like all other elements of your marketing campaign – needs to have clear goals and objectives. Creating brand and product awareness will not happen overnight so it is important to budget accordingly, ensuring there is money set aside for maintenance of the website and analytics.

Be flexible with ideas and options—do your research first, try out different options, then test and measure the results. Metrics and evaluations can be updated almost immediately and should be monitored regularly. By keeping an eye out for what online marketing strategies are working and which are not, it will be easier to create a balanced portfolio of marketing techniques. You might find that in certain geographical areas, certain marketing strategies are more effective than others.

This list is by no means the full extent of options available for marketing online, but it is a good place to start when deciding which options are best suited to your company.

Create a website

The primary use for the internet is information seeking, so you should provide consumers with information about your company first hand. You have more control over your branding and messaging and can also collect visitor information to determine what types of internet users are accessing your website.

Search Engine Optimization

Since search engines comprise 50% of the most visited sites globally, you can go through your website to make it more search engine friendly with the aim to increase your organic search listing. An organic search listing refers to listings in search engine results that appear in order or relevance to the entered search terms.

You may wish to repeat key words multiple times throughout your website and write the copy on your site not only with the end reader in mind, but also search engines.

Remember when you design your website that any text that appears in Flash format can now be recognized by Google but may not be recognized by other search engines. If your entire website is built on a Flash platform, you may have a poor organic search listing.

Price Per Click Advertising

If you find that visitors access your website after searching for it first on a search engine, then it may be beneficial to advertise on these websites and bid on keywords associated with your company.

These advertisements will appear at the top of the page or along the left side of the search results on a search engine. You can have control over the specific geographic area you wish to target, set a monthly budget and have the option to only be charged when a user clicks on your link.

Online Directories

Listing your business in an online directory can be an inexpensive and effective online marketing strategy.

However, you need to be able to distinguish your company from the plethora of competitors that may exist. Likely, you will need to complement this strategy with other brand awareness campaigns.

Online Ads (i.e. banner ads on other websites)

These advertisements can have positive or negative effects based on the reputation and consumer perception of the website on which you are advertising. These ads should be treated similar to print ads you may place in local newspapers or other publications.

Online Videos

With the growing popularity of sites such as You Tube, it is evident that people love researching online and being able to find video clips of the information they are seeking. Depending on your small business, you may want to upload informational videos or tutorials about your products or services.

Blogging

Blogging can be a fun and interactive way to communicate with users. A blog is traditionally a website maintained by an individual user that has regular entries, similar to a diary. These entries can be commentaries, descriptions of events, pictures, videos, and more. Companies can use blogging as a way to keep users updated on current information and allow them to post comments on your blog. If blogging is something you wish to invest in, make sure that it is regularly updated and monitored.

TOP 10 MISTAKES TO AVOID

Failure to measure ROI

Which metrics are you using? Are your visitors actually motivated to purchase or sign up? If the benefits of your online campaign are not greater than the costs incurred, then you may wish to re-evaluate your strategy.

Poor Web Design

This can leave a poor impression of your company on the visitor. A poor design could result in frustration on the visitors' part if they are not able to easily find what they went on your site to search for and also does not build trust. If consumers do not trust your company or your website, you will not be able to complete the sale and develop a longer relationship with that customer. You also need to include privacy protection and security when building trust.

This also includes ensuring all information on the website is current and having customer service available if users are experiencing difficulty or cannot find the information they are seeking. This could be as simple as providing a 'Contact Us' email or phone number for support.

Becoming locked into an advertising strategy early

Remember your marketing mix when creating a marketing strategy and avoid putting all of your eggs in one basket. Online marketing is a very valuable tool, but depending on your business and your target markets, other marketing campaigns may be the best option for you. Especially if this is your first time making a significant investment into your online sector, you want to remain flexible and able to adapt your strategy based off feedback received by researching and analyzing different options.

Acting without researching

Similar to becoming locked into an advertising strategy early, this mistake implies not dutifully testing and researching different online marketing options. For example, if your target consumer is age 65+ and you are spending all of your marketing efforts into creating a blogging website (where the average ages of bloggers are 18-35), then you are likely not going to have a successful campaign.

Assuming more visitors means more sales

You have to go back to your original goals and the purpose of your company. More visitors may not mean more sales if your website is used primarily for information and consumers purchase their products elsewhere. This is also vice versa. You could have an increase in sales without an increase in unique visitors if your current consumer base is very loyal and willing to spend lots of money.

Often people will collect information online about products they wish to purchase because it is easier to compare options, but they purchase in person. Even though shopping online is becoming quite popular, people still prefer to see and feel the physical product before purchasing.

Failing to follow up with customers that purchase

Repeat sales can account for up to 60% of total revenue. It's no wonder that organizations are always trying to maintain loyal customers and may have customer relationship management systems in place. It is easier to get a happy customer to purchase again than it is to get a new customer to purchase once.

Not incorporating online marketing into the business plan

By ensuring that your online marketing plan is fully integrated and accurately represents your organization's overall goals and objectives, the business plan will need to be more comprehensive and encompassing.

Trying to discover your own best practices

It is very beneficial to use trial and error to determine the best online strategy from your company, but do not be afraid to do your research and learn from what others have already figured out. There will be many cases where someone was in a very similar position as you and they may have some suggestions and secrets that they wish to share. Researching in advance can save a great deal of time and money.

Spending too much too fast

Although it may be cheaper than traditional marketing approaches, internet marketing does have its costs. You have to consider the software and hardware designs, maintenance, distribution, supply chain management, and the time that will be required. You don't want to spend your entire marketing budget all at once.

Getting distracted by metrics that are not relevant

As discussed in the following section, there are endless reports and measurables that you can analyze to determine the effectiveness of your campaign. You will need to establish which measurables are actually relevant to your marketing.

TESTING AND MEASURING ONLINE

As with any element of your marketing campaign, you will need to track your results and measure them against your investment. Otherwise, how will you know if your online marketing is successful?

These results - or metrics – need to be recorded and analyzed as to how they impact your overall return on investment.

Some examples of metrics are:

- New account setups

- Conversion rates

- Page stickiness

- Contact us form completion

Due to the popularity in online marketing and the importance of having a strong web presence, companies have demanded more sophisticated tracking tools and metrics for their online activities. It can be very difficult to not only know what to measure, but also HOW to measure.

Thankfully, it is easier than ever to get the information you need with the many types of software and services available, including Google Analytics, which are free and relatively accurate.

8 Metrics to Track

The following are the key measurables to watch for when testing and measuring your internet marketing efforts:

Conversions

How many leads has your online presence generated, and of those leads, how many were turned into sales? Ultimately, your campaign needs to have a positive impact on your business.

Regardless of the specific purpose of the campaign – from lead generation and service sign-up, to blog entries – you need to know how many customers are taking the desired action in response to your efforts. Your tracking tool will be able to provide you with this information

Spend

If you are not making a profit – or at least breaking even – from your internet marketing efforts, then you need to change your strategy. Redistribute your financial resources and reconsider your motives and objectives for your online campaign.

An easy way to do this analysis is to divide your total spend by conversions. This could also be broken down by product. You could also use a tracking tool and view reports on the 'per visit value of every click,' from every source. Your sources can include organic/search engine referrals, direct visit (i.e. person typed your web address into their address bar), or email/newsletter.

Attention

You need to keep a close eye on how much attention you are getting on your website. One of the best ways to analyze this would be to compare unique visitors to page views per visit to time on site. How many people are visiting, how many pages they are viewing, what pages they are viewing, and how much time they are spending on the site.

A unique visitor is any one person who visits the website in a given amount of time. For example, if Evelyn visits her online banking website daily for an entire month, over that one month period, she is considered to be one unique visitor (not 30 visitors).

You may also want to incorporate referring source as well – the places online that refer customers to your website. You'll be able to determine what referring sources offer the 'best' visitors.

Top Referrals

Know who is doing the best job of referring clients to your website – and note how they are doing this. Is it the prominence of the link? Positioning? Reputation of the referring company?

Understanding where the majority of your visitors are coming from will allow you focus on those types of sources when you increase your referral sites. They also allow you to gain a better understanding of your online market – and target audience.

Bounce Rate

The bounce rate is the number of people who visit the homepage of your website, but do not visit other pages. If you have a high bounce rate, you either have all the necessary information on your homepage, or you are not giving your customers a reason to click further.

In Google Analytics, view the 'content' or 'pages' report and view the column stating bounce rate.

Errors

It is very important to track the errors that visitors receive while trying to access or view your website. For example, if someone links to your website, but makes a spelling error in typing the link, your users will see an error page in their browser, and will not ultimately make it to your website.

You can also receive reports on errors that customer's make when trying to type in your website address in their browser. You may wish to buy the domains with common spelling mistakes, and link those addresses to your true homepage. This will increase overall traffic and potential conversions.

Onsite Search Terms

If you have a 'search website' function on your website, it is useful to monitor which terms users are most frequently searching. This can provide valuable insight into the user friendliness of your site and your website's navigation system. This information will be included in the traffic reporting tool.

Bailout Rates

If you provide users with the option to purchase something on your website (i.e. shopping cart), then you can track where along the purchasing process people decided not to go through with the sale.

This could be at the first step of receiving the order summary and total, or further when stating shipping options. By obtaining this information, a company can reorganize or revamp their website to make the sales process more fluid and possibly encourage more purchases.

Here are the three main questions you should be asking yourself when evaluating your website presence:

- Who visits my website?

- Where do visitors come from?

- Which pages are viewed?

Use Scripts
to Increase Sales
Immediately

✦ ✦ ✦

What do playbooks, prompts, guides and scripts all have in common?

They are all popular tools that dictate or guide human behavior toward a desired outcome.

Playbooks help coaches tell sports teams specifically how to play the game to overcome an opponent. Prompts help to kick-start writers and other creative professionals when stuck in a rut. Guides provide a series of instructions so that a person or team of people can complete or implement a specific task. Film scripts tell actors how to act for a particular part.

If you're in the business of sales, you also know about sales scripts. Sales scripts are tools that guide salespeople during interactions or conversations with potential customers.

A large number of businesses use scripts, either as a way of maintaining consistency amongst a sales team, training new salespeople, or enhancing their sales skills. They may have a single script, or several, and may change their scripts regularly, or use the same one for years.

What most businesses overlook, however, is that the sales script is a living, breathing, changing member of their sales team. They may be internal documents, but they deserve just as much time and effort as your marketing collateral.

DO YOU REALLY NEED A SCRIPT?

The short answer is yes. You absolutely need a script for any and every customer interaction you and your salespeople may find yourselves in.

Sure, countless business owners and salespeople work every day without a script. If you own your own business, chances are you're already a pretty good salesperson. But if you are not using scripts, you're only working at half of your true potential – or half of your potential earnings.

Scripts don't have to be "cheesy" or read verbatim. They act as a map for your sales process, and provide prompts to trigger your memory and keep you on track. How many times have you made a cold call that didn't work out the way you wanted it to? Scripts dramatically improve the effectiveness and efficiency of your sales processes.

A comprehensive set of scripts will also keep a level of consistency amongst your salespeople and the customer service they provide your clients.

Once scripts are written, memorized, and rehearsed, they become like film scripts; the salesperson can breathe their own life and personality into the conversation, while staying focused on the call's objectives.

WHY YOUR SCRIPTS AREN'T WORKING

If you a currently using scripts in your business, are they working? Are they as effective as they could possibly be? How do you know? When was the last time they were reviewed or updated?

Scripts are like any other element of your marketing campaign – they need to be tested and measured for results, and changed based on what is or is not working.

Measure the success of your script based on your conversion rates. Of all the people you speak to and use the script, how many are being converted from leads to sales?

When evaluating your existing scripts, ask yourself the following questions:

How old is this script? What was it written for? Scripts are living, breathing members of your company. They need to be written and rewritten and rewritten again as the needs of your customers change, your product or services change, or as new strategies are implemented.

Does this script address all the customer objections we regularly hear? Every time you hear a customer raise an objection that is not included on the script, add it. The power of your script lies in the ability to anticipate customer concerns, and answer them before they're raised.

Does this script sound the same as the others? Your scripts are part of the package that represents you as a company. There should be a consistent feel or approach throughout your scripts that your customers will recognize and feel confident dealing with.

Is everyone using the script? Who on your team regularly uses these scripts? Just the junior staff? Only the top-performing staff? Make sure everyone is singing from the same song sheet – your customers will appreciate the consistency.

TYPES OF SCRIPTS

Depending on the product or service you offer and the marketing strategies you have chosen, there are countless types of scripts you could potentially prepare for your business,

When you sit down to create your scripts, it would be wise to start by making a list of all the instances you and your staff members interact with your existing or potential customers. Then, prioritize the list from most to least important, and start writing from the top.

Here are some commonly used scripts, and their purposes:

Sales presentation script

Each time you or your sales staff make a presentation, they should be using the same or a slightly modified version of the same script. This script will include sample icebreakers, a presentation on benefits and features of the product or service, and a list of possible objections and responses. These scripts should also help alleviate some of the nervousness or anxiety associated with public speaking.

Closing script

Closing scripts help you do just that: close the sale. This could include a list of closing prompts or statements to get the transaction started. This type of script also includes a list of possible customer objections, and planned responses.

Incoming phone call script

Everyone who calls your business should be treated the same way; consistent information should be gathered and provided to the customer. The person answering the phone should state the company name, department name, and their own name in the initial greeting. This goes for both the main line, and each individual or department extension.

Cold call script

This is one of the most important scripts you can perfect for your business. The cold call script must master the art of quickly getting the attention of the customer, then engaging and persuading them with the benefits of the product or service. The caller needs to establish common ground with the potential customer, and find a way to get them talking through open-ended questions.

Direct mail follow-up script

Scripts for outgoing calls that are intended to follow up on a direct mail piece are essential for every direct mail campaign. They are designed to call qualified leads that have already received information and an offer, and convert them into customers. These scripts should focus on enticing customers to act, and overcoming any objections that may have prevented them from acting sooner.

Market research script

Scripts that are used primarily for the purpose of gathering information should be designed to get the customer talking. A focus on open-ended questions and relationship building statements will help to relax the customer, and encourage honest dialogue.

Difficult customer script

Just like every salesperson needs to practice the sales process, you and your staff also need to practice your ability to handle difficult customers. If you operate a retail business this is especially important, as difficult customers often present themselves in front of other customers. These scripts should help you diffuse the situation, calm the customer down, and then handle their objections.

CREATING SCRIPTS

Creating powerful scripts is not a complicated exercise, but it will take some time to complete. Focus on the most vital scripts for your business first, and engage the assistance of your sales staff in drafting or reviewing the scripts.

YOUR SCRIPT BINDER

Keep master copies of all of your scripts in one organized place. An effective way to do this is to create a binder, and use tabs to separate each type of script.

You will also want to create a separate tab for customer objections, and list every single customer objection you have ever heard in relation to your product or service. Find a way to organize each objection so you can easily find them – group them by category or separate them with tabs.

Then, list your responses next to each objection – there should be several responses to each objection created with different customer types in mind. A master list of customer objections and responses is an invaluable tool for any business owner, salesperson, and script writer. The more responses you can think of, the better.

Remember, the script binder is never "finished." You will need to make sure that it is updated and added to on a regular basis.

WRITING SCRIPTS – STEP BY STEP

STEP ONE: Record What You're Doing Now

If you aren't using scripts – or even if you are – start by recording yourself in action. Use video or audio recording to tape yourself on the phone, in a sales presentation, or with a customer.

Make notes on your body language, word choice, customer reaction and body language, responses to objections, and closing statements.

You may also wish to ask an associate to make notes on your performance and discuss them with you in a constructive fashion.

STEP TWO: Evaluate What You're Doing Wrong

Take a look at your notes, and ask yourself the following questions:

+ How are you engaging the customer?

+ Are you building common ground and trust?

+ Does what you are saying matter to the customer?

+ Is your offer a powerful one?

+ What objections are raised?

+ How are you dealing with them?

+ What objections are you avoiding?

+ How natural is your close?

+ Are you as effective as you think you can be?

Once you have answered and made notes in response to these questions, make a list of things you need to improve, and how you think you might go about doing so. Do you need to strengthen your closing statements? Do you need to brainstorm more responses to objections? Remember that everyone's script and sales process can be improved.

STEP THREE: Decide Who the Script is For

So now that you know the elements of your script you need to work on, you can begin drafting your new script, or revising an old one.

The first part of writing a script – or any piece of marketing material – is having a strong understanding of who you are writing it for. Who is your target audience? What does your ideal customer look like? Consider demographic characteristics like age, sex, location, income, occupation and marital status. Be as specific as possible. What are their purchase patterns? What motivates them to spend money?

If you are writing a cold call script, you will need to develop or purchase a list of people who fall into the target market specifics you have established. If you are writing a sales script for in-store customers, then spend some time reviewing what types of customers find their way into your place of business.

You will want to use words that your target audience will not only understand, but relate to and resonate with. Use sensory language that will trigger emotional and feeling responses – I need this, this will solve that problem, I'll feel better if I have this, etc.

STEP FOUR: Decide What You Want to Say

There are typically five sections of every script – and there may be more, depending on the type and purpose of the script:

1. **Engage**

    + Get their attention or pique their interest

    + Establish common ground

    + Build trust, be human

    + Ask for their time

2. **Ask + Qualify**

    + Take control of the conversation by asking questions

    + Focus on open-ended questions that cannot be answered with a "yes" or "no"

    + Get the customer talking

    + Ask as many questions as you need to get information on the customer's needs and purchase motivations

3. Get Agreement

- Ask closed-ended questions you are sure they will respond with "yes"
- Get them to agree on the benefits of the product or service
- Repeat key points back to the customer to gain agreement

4. Overcome Objections

- Anticipate objections based on customer comments, then refute them
- Make informative assumptions about their thought process, identify with their concern, then refute it using your own experiences
- Repeat concerns back to the customer to let them know you have heard them
- Ask about any remaining objections before you close

5. Close

- Assume that you have overcome all objections, and have the sale
- Ask the customer transactional questions, like delivery timing and payment method
- Be as confident and natural as possible

STEP FIVE: Train Your Staff

Once you have written your company's scripts, you will need to ensure your staff understands and are comfortable using them.

Consider having a team meeting, and use role play to review each of the scripts. This will encourage your salespeople to practice amongst each other, and strengthen their sales skills. Ask them for feedback on the scripts, and make any necessary changes.

You will also need to decide how comfortable you are having your salespeople personalizing the scripts to suit their own styles. Be clear what elements of the script are "company standards" and essential techniques, but also be flexible with your team.

STEP SIX: Continually Revise

After you have carefully crafted your script, put it to the test. Practice on your colleagues, friends, and family. Get their feedback, and make changes.

Remember that scripts will need to change and evolve as your business changes and evolves, and new products or services are introduced. Keep your script binder on your desk at all times, and continually make changes and improvements to it.

You may also wish to record and evaluate your performance on a regular basis. This is an exercise you could incorporate into regular employee reviews, and use as a constructive tool for staff development.

SCRIPT TIPS

+ Practice anticipating and eliciting real objections – including the ones your customer doesn't want to raise.

+ Make the script yours – it should look, feel, and sound like you naturally do, not like you're reading off the page.

+ Spend time with the masters. If there is a salesperson you admire in your community, ask to observe them in action. Take notes on their performance, and the techniques they use for success.

+ If your script is not successful, ask the customer why not? Even if you don't get the sale, you'll get a new objection you can craft responses to and never get stumped by it again.

+ Don't fear objections. Just spend time identifying as many as possible, then practice overcoming them.

+ Never stop thinking of responses to customer objections. Each objection could potentially have 30 responses, geared toward specific customer types.

+ Anecdotes are persuasive writing tools – use them in your scripts. People enjoy hearing stories, especially stories that relate to them and their experiences, frustrations, and troubles. Let the story sell your product or service for you.

+ Include body language in your scripts – it's just as important as your words. Try mimicking your subject's posture, arm position, and seating position. This is proven to create ease and build trust.

+ If you only have your voice, use it. Pay attention to tone, language choice, speed, and background noise. You only have sound to establish a trusting relationships, so do it carefully.

+ Be confident, and focus on a positive stream of self-talk to prepare for the call or presentation. Confidence sells.

+ Spend time on your closing scripts, as they are a critical component of your presentation or phone call. This can be a challenging part of the sales process, so practice, practice, practice.

How to Create Repeat Business and have Clients that Pay, Stay and Refer

✦ ✦ ✦

When it comes to marketing and generating more income, most business owners are focused outward.

They've carefully established and segmented their target market, and created specific offers and messages for each market segment. They spend thousands of dollars in advertising and direct mail campaigns in hot pursuit of more leads, more customers, and more foot traffic.

While this is an effective way to build a business, it is costly and time consuming. It requires constant and consistent effort, and while this approach does generate results, those results quickly disappear when the effort stops or becomes less intense.

Successful businesses that see sustained growth have a double-edged marketing strategy. They focus their efforts *outward* – on new potential customers and marketing – as well as *inward* – on existing customers and referral business.

These successful businesses have leveraged their existing efforts to generate more revenue. Simply put, their customers buy from them over and over again.

For most businesses, this is the easiest way to increase their revenues. Simple customer loyalty strategies and outstanding customer service are often all you need to dramatically increase your sales – from the customers you already have.

THE COST OF YOUR CUSTOMERS

Do you know how much it costs your business to buy new customers?

Each new customer that walks through your door – with the exception of referrals – has cost you money to acquire. You have spent money on advertising and promotions to generate leads and turn those leads into customers.

For example, if you have placed an ad in your local newspaper for $1,000, and the ad brings in 10 customers, you have paid $100 to acquire each customer. You would need to ensure each of those customers spent at least $200 to cover your cost of goods or services sold to break even (assuming the cost of your product or service is also $100). This is why it is imperative that you know your customer acquisition cost and your gross profit (see page 62 on calculating gross profit).

Alternately, if you spent two hours of your time and $10 per month on an email marketing program to send a newsletter to your existing database of customers, and you bring in 10 customers as a result – each customer has cost you $1. Generating more repeat business means focusing on the marketing strategies that aim to keep your existing customers instead of purchase new ones – effectively reducing the cost of attracting new customers to your business.

These strategies are simple to implement, and don't require much time investment. Just a solid understanding of how to make customers want to come back and spend more of their money.

KEEPING YOUR CUSTOMERS

Marketing strategies that focus on keeping your current customer base are easy and enjoyable to implement. They allow you to build real relationships with the people you do business with, instead of dealing with a revolving door of people on the other end of your sales process.

Repeat customers create a community of people around your business that presumably share the same needs, desires and frustrations. The information you gain from these customers (market research) can help you strengthen your understanding of your target audience, and more accurately segment it.

Remember – 80% of your revenue comes from 20% of your customers (again this percentage may vary some depending on your type of business). Always focus on these customers. They are ideal customers that you want to recruit, and hold on to.

Customer Service: Make them love buying from you

Every business – even those with excellent service standards can improve the service they provide their customers. Customer service seems to be a dying concept in most businesses; more focus seems to be placed on the speed of the transaction. These days you can even go to the grocery store now and not speak to a single sales associate, thanks to self-serve checkouts.

To improve your company's customer service standards, take a survey of your customers and your employees to brainstorm ways you can improve the experience of buying from your business.

Successful customer service standards – those that make your customers buy – are:

Consistent. The standards are kept up by every person in your organization. Expectations are clear and followed through. Customers know what to expect, and choose your business because of those expectations.

Convenient. It is nearly effortless for the customer to spend money at your place of business. Convenience can take many forms – location, product selection, value-added services like delivery – and it is also consistent.

Customer-driven. The service the customer receives is exactly how they would like to be treated when buying your product or service. It is reflective of your target market, and appropriate to their lifestyle. Customers would probably not appreciate white linen tablecloths at a fast food restaurant, but they would appreciate a 2-minute or less guarantee.

Newsletters: Keep in touch with your customers

A regular newsletter is an easy, time-effective, and inexpensive marketing strategy to implement. Unfortunately, many small businesses think these are too time consuming and too expensive to adopt as part of their marketing strategy.

The most popular type of newsletter distribution is email. This will cost your business as little at $10 per month for an email marketing service subscription, and can be customized to your unique branding.

Here is an easy five-step process to starting a company newsletter:

1. **Pick your audience.** New customers? Market segment? Existing customers?

2. **Choose what you're going to say.** Company news? Feature product? New offer?

3. **Determine how you're going to say it.** Articles? Bullet points? Pictures?

4. **Decide how it's going to get to your audience.** Email? Mail? In-store?

5. **Track your results.** How many people opened it? Read it? Took action?

Value Added Service: Give them happy surprises

Adding value to your business is an effective way of getting your customers back. Every person I know would choose a mattress store that offered free delivery over one that did not. It's that simple.

There are many ways to add value to your business, including:

- **Feature your expertise.** Use your knowledge to provide additional value to your customers. Offer a free consumer guide or report with every purchase.

- **Add convenience services.** Offer a service that makes their purchase easier, or more convenient. The best example of this is free shipping or delivery.

- **Package complementary services.** Packaging like items together creates an increase in perceived value. This is great for start-up kits.

- **Offer new products or services.** Feature top of the line or exclusive products, available only at your business. Offer a new service or profile a new staff member with niche expertise.

Value added services generate repeat customers in one of two ways:

1. **Impress them on their first visit.** Impress your customer with great service, a product that meets their needs, and then wow them with something extra that they weren't expecting. Get them to associate the experience of dealing with your business with happy surprises, and create a perception of higher value.

2. **Entice them to come back.** The introduction of a new value-added service can be enough to convince a customer to buy from you again. Their initial purchase established a trust and knowledge of your business and its processes. They will want to "be included" in anything new you have to offer – especially if there is exclusivity. It is easier to attract

clients that have purchased from you than potential clients who have not.

Customer Loyalty Programs: Give them incentives

Another simple way to keep in touch with existing customers and keep them coming back to you is to create a customer loyalty program.

These programs do not have to be complicated or costly, and are relatively easy to maintain once they have been implemented. These programs help you gain more information on your customers and their purchasing habits.

Here are some examples of simple loyalty programs that you can implement:

+ **Free product or service.** Give them every 10th (or 6th) product or service free. Produce stamp cards with your logo and contact information on it.

+ **Reward dollars.** Give them a certain percentage of their purchase back in money that can only be spent in-store. Produce "funny money" with your logo and brand.

+ **Rewards points.** Give them a certain number of points for every dollar they spend. These points can be spent in-store, or on special items you bring in for points only.

+**Membership amenities.** Give members access to VIP amenities that are not available to other customers. Produce member cards or give out member numbers.

Remember that in order for this strategy to work, you and your team have to understand and promote it. The program in itself becomes a product that you sell.

Profits from
Fresh Air

+ + +

As a small business owner, you are in business for one reason: to make money.

Of course, there are other reasons you started or purchased your company. You may love the product you sell, or service you provide. You may love the challenge of turning a floundering company into an overnight success. You may just love being your own boss.

Naturally, this all means nothing if you are not generating enough income to support yourself and your family, as well as the people who work for you.

Nearly all businesses make money. Unless not a single product or service is sold, there is always money coming in. But there is also always money going out. Supplies, wages, marketing, acquisitions and operations all contribute to the expense of just staying in business.

Simply put, profit is the difference between money in and money out. This is the dollar value of your sales, minus the cost of those sales.

In business, you will find that everyone wants to make more money. They want to increase their sales, get more money coming in. **What often gets overlooked is that the true secret to making more money is not increasing sales, but increasing profit.**

WHAT IS PROFIT?

Before you can take steps to increase the profitability of your business, you have to have a solid understanding of:

+ types of profit

+ what factors influence profit

+ what your profit is right now

Types of Profit

There are two main types of profit:

Gross Profit

Gross profit is the simplest form of calculating profit. It is simply the money that comes through the cash register, minus the cost of acquiring or providing the products or services.

The formula is:

Total revenue (sales) – cost of goods or services sold = Gross Profit

Net Profit

Net profit is a more accurate reflection of your income. It is calculated by taking your gross profit minus expenses over a specific time period (usually by month or by quarter).

The formula is:

Gross profit – expenses (cost of running a business) = Net Profit

Factors that Influence Profit

Profit is your bottom line. It is the number that falls out the bottom when all other costs and expenses have been taken into consideration. Do you know what contributes to the amount of profit your business ends up with?

There are three main factors that influence profit:

Sales – Your Conversion Rate

The first, and most obvious, factor is the money that comes in the door through sales. In theory, the more sales you make, the more money you bring in, the greater your profits.

The ratio of potential customers to sales is called your conversion rate. This is the percentage of customers you have converted from leads to sales. So, a high conversion rate means more sales, and more money coming in the door.

In addition to your conversion rate is the lifetime value of your clients. It costs much less to convince a customer to make repeat purchases than it does to acquire new clients.

Costs – Your Product/Service Margins

The second factor is the cost of your offering – what your product or service costs you to acquire or provide. If you sell a product, this is the wholesale price you pay for the product. If you offer a service, it is the cost of your (or your employee's) time plus any materials used.

Your margin is the difference between the price you pay and the price your customers pay. If you buy toothpaste for $1 from the wholesaler, and you sell it for $3, your margin is $2. If a haircut costs $20 in materials and service, and the customer pays $50, your margin is $30.

Expenses – The Cost of Doing Business

The final factor is the cost of running your business – those not directly related to the specific product or service you offer. Expenses include:

+ Office or store lease

+ Computer equipment lease

+ Employee salaries

+ Utilities

+ Marketing + advertising

Your Profit

It only makes sense that you need to know where you are to determine how to get to where you want to be. This applies to any plan you create in business.

Before you can increase your profits, you need to have an understanding of where your profits are currently – and if you're making any at all. The next section will take you through a process to review the specific factors that affect your business's profitability, and ultimately determine how much profit you are currently bringing in.

TAKING STOCK OF YOUR PROFITS

Before you devise a strategy to increase your profits, you need to take a good long look at the money your business brings in, and the money you spend to run your business. You may wish to sit down with your accountant or bookkeeper to analyze the financial information that is available to you.

Decide on a specific time period to review – one that makes sense to your business, and one that will give you the most realistic picture of your business performance.

This will depend on whether your operation is cyclical, or remains steady throughout the year. Usually, the previous quarter or the previous four quarters will give you enough of an indication.

Here is a general of items to review:

+ Total revenue

+ Total cost of goods or services

+ Total cost of operations (overhead), including:

+ Employee wages

+ Recruitment

+ Business development

+ Utilities

- Rent or mortgage

- Office supplies

- Computer leases

- Incidentals

- Total cost of marketing campaigns

Total profit after costs and expenses for this time period: _____ .

THE FIVE FACTORS THAT EAT YOUR PROFITS

It is easy for business owners to compare their organizations to the apparent success of their competitors. Joe's Pizza may always be overflowing with customers and appear to be making money hand over fist, while your pizza shop may have slower, but more steady business.

It is important to remember that a business with extraordinary sales figures is not necessarily a profitable one. Sales are just one element of your profit calculation. Here are some other elements to think about when reviewing the profitability of your business:

Impulse Spending

How often do you make purchases for your business operations? I'm not talking about acquiring new goods and services, but upgrading computers, taking your team out for lunch, or leasing a new color photocopier.

Do you allow your staff to make purchases on your behalf? Who reviews these decisions? Take a look not only at what you buy, but how spending is structured in your company.

Small Margins

As we discussed in the previous section, your margins are the difference between your cost and the customer's cost to purchase your goods or services.

Typically, businesses that offer a variety of products will have both products with large margins, and products with small margins. The products with large margins generate the most income, so these are the products that staff should be focused on selling.

What many businesses overlook is that products with small margins will never generate a high level of income, no matter how many you sell. A store stocked with small margin items will never be able to increase their profit because they have so little margin to work with.

Your Customers

This may seem like a backwards way of thinking. Your customers spend money, so they are a positive factor in your profit calculation, right?

This is true for most of your customers. But remember the 80/20 rule of business – 80% of your revenue comes from 20% of your customers. These are your top 20%, or ideal customers. What about your bottom 20%? The group of clients who ask for the moon and never stop complaining.

These clients can be a huge drain on both your staff resources and your financial resources. Their true value to your business is minimal – they cost more than they bring in. Fire them and spend your resources servicing your ideal customers, finding more ideal customers, or turning the other 60% into ideal customers!

Loan Interest

How many business loans do you currently have? Credit card debt? Overdraft? The interest you pay on these loans can be a substantial monthly cost to your business.

A loan from a bank is just like any other product. You can shop around for the best deal. Consider consolidating or restructuring your debt to minimize interest payments. Plan to search around for the best rate on a regular basis – every few months or quarter.

Vendors

Do you purchase your goods and services from a wholesaler or retailer? How long have you been in business with this company? What do you pay for goods and services relative to your competitors?

Ensure that you are dealing with as direct a vendor as possible to minimize your acquisition costs and increase your margins. If you have been doing business with a particular vendor for an extended period of time, consider renegotiating your business arrangement.

THE BASICS OF INCREASING PROFIT

Your Profitability Goal

Now that you have an understanding of the current profitability of your company, it is time to look at ways to increase your bottom line.

Like all other aspects of your business development, you need to have a clear idea of your intention or purpose before you begin any activity. Assuming you wish to increase the profitability of your business, you need to determine by how much and within what time frame (Review Chapter 1 on Goal Setting).

Create a profit-related goal for your business, and write it here:

_____

_____

Three Ways to Increase Profit

There are countless strategies for increasing profit, but ultimately you can only increase profit in one of three ways:

1. Get More Customers

Use marketing outreach strategies to generate more leads, and convert those leads into more customers. Introduce a new offer, expand your target audience, or approach a new target audience.

2. Get Your Customers to Buy More Often

Use customer loyalty and retention strategies to get your existing customers to buy from you more often. Make it easy for them to come back and do business with you.

You can do this by adding value to your product or service, keeping in touch on a regular basis, and giving your customers incentive to make repeat purchases. Customer service is also an overlooked component of building a repeat client base.

3. Increase How Much Your Customers Buy

You'll naturally increase your sales when you increase the number of customers and how often they purchase. The final way you can impact your profit is by increasing the average dollar value of each sale.

This can be achieved by up-selling every customer, creating package offers, and finding ways to increase the perceived value of your offering to justify increasing the price.

MANAGING COSTS

One important way to impact the profitability of your business is through cost or spending management. Controlling how much money goes out will help you ensure that a more money stays in your bank account.

Remember, however, that cutting costs can only help increase your profits so much. There is a point where you will no longer be able to reduce expenses, and you will have to focus on increasing sales.

Why Cut Costs?

Cost management may seem like an obvious way of maintaining a healthy business, but it is also one of the primary reasons 80% of small businesses fail. Overspending is a huge problem for most businesses – and they don't even realize it.

Reducing costs is a great short-term strategy to boost profits. As I mentioned above, there is a limited amount of impact cost management can have on the bottom line, so it is an ineffective long term strategy.

Cost management can also help you to generate more capital. A business that closely monitors and controls its spending is a much more desirable loan candidate than a business that spends freely.

Most importantly, this strategy will help keep your business profitable through high and low periods. It's easy to spend money when your company is doing well, but this leaves little in the "emergency fund" account for downturns in the economy or unexpected expenses.

WHERE CAN I CUT COSTS?

Financing

As I mentioned, interest rates are a big culprit when it comes to eating profits. Take stock of how much money you are spending on a monthly basis in loan and interest payments. Can this be reduced? Is there another bank that will offer you a lower rate? Is there a way to consolidate these loans into a single, low-interest account?

Alternatively, if your business is doing well and has a large amount of money sitting in the bank; consider investing it or placing it in a high-interest savings account (Although today's interest rates are at historical lows, this will not last forever). The point is let your money make you money instead of spending it on unnecessary business luxuries.

Suppliers or Vendors

Again, as mentioned above, make sure the price you pay for goods and services – for resale or internal use – is the lowest you can find. Try to deal directly with the manufacturer or distributor, and renegotiate discounts and contracts with your vendors every year.

Hours of Operation

Evaluate the hours you are open for business each day, and why you have chosen the specific timeframe. Is it to compete with the competitors? Is it because you can serve the highest number of customers? Each hour you are open for business costs you money, so make sure you are operating under the most ideal timeframe.

Staffing, Wages, and Compensation

This can be a sensitive subject for any business owner or employee. It is important to look at staffing redundancies and capacity levels – as well as hiring needs – when evaluating cost management strategies.

Do you need to hire new staff, or can you build capacity within your existing employees? Is there another way to compensate staff, or provide performance incentives that are non-monetary, have a high perceived value, and inexpensive for your business? Remember to take time and care when implementing any changes in this area of cost management.

Place of Business

If you operate an office in a downtown metropolis, you are going to have substantially higher operating costs than a competitor who runs an office just outside the city limits.

Make sure you can justify your location, and the amount of money you spend to be there. Consider the following questions:

- Are my customers impacted by where I do business?
- Do my customers need to visit my office?
- What impression does my business need to present?
- Do I need parking facilities?
- Do I need to be visible?
- Do I have staff to employ?
- Am I near public transit, lunch outlets, and other amenities?
- Do I need access after business hours?
- Should I lease or buy?
- What other costs are specific to this location?

Eliminate the invisible!

What could you and your staff live without? What wouldn't you notice if it just disappeared one day? Take stock of expenses that are not being properly used or appreciated. Think of amenity-based items, or convenience costs, like:

- Gym Memberships
- Morning refreshments (muffins, donuts, etc.)
- Publication Subscriptions
- Designer coffee and tea
- Fancy collateral packaging

All cost reduction decisions are not only about the numbers. You need to consider the unintended consequences of these decisions, the value of long term vendor relationships and the impact those consequences may have on employee morale and customer perception.

YOUR PRICING STRATEGY

The cost of your goods and services have a direct impact on the money you bring in. Your pricing strategy is so important to your business that it can even determine your success.

Deciding how much to charge for your product or service is a challenging task. You need to factor in your own costs, the product or service's perceived value, and the going rate. Ultimately, you want to be able to charge as much as possible for each item, without overpricing yourself out of business.

Avoid the Lowest Pricing Strategy

The days of the lowest price guarantee and pricing wars are over – especially for small businesses. The "big players" in the marketplace will quickly put you out of business if you try to compete on price. Their pockets are deeper and they have lower operating costs due to their sheer size. They can afford to – you can't.

Clearly Position Your Company and Your Offering

How do you want your target market to view your business, and your products? Are you trying to create an image of high quality? High value? Reliable service? Make sure your pricing is consistent with the image you are trying to project. If you are operating a high end spa – you're not competing with the budget nail salon down the street, so your prices should be considerably higher.

Have a Good Working Understanding of Your Margins

Know how much the product or service costs you to offer before you establish a price. Do these costs remain consistent, or do they fluctuate? Restaurants that offer high quality meat and seafood often price their meals at "market rates" as opposed to fixed rates. Calculate the fixed and variable costs associated with your product or service. You will want to work the cost of the product or service, a percentage of your overhead, and your own profit into the cost of each item.

Pay Attention to Factors Beyond Your Control

Be aware of any government or industry regulations on the price of your product or services. Some laws will actually limit how much you can charge for standard services. For medical and dental services, most insurance companies will put a cap on how much a customer will be compensated for each service. Seek out all external factors that could impact your pricing.

Price with a Purpose

Your pricing strategy should be purpose focused. What exactly are you trying to do by setting your prices at certain levels? Here are some potential reasons for pricing strategies:

+ Short-term profit increase

+ Long-term profit increase

+ Customer generation

+ Product positioning

+ Revenue maximization

+ Increase margins

+ Market differentiation

+ Survival

PRICING STRATEGIES

Cost Plus Pricing

This is the most basic pricing strategy. Set your price at a number that includes:

+ Cost of goods or services, based on a specific sales volume

+ Percentage of expenses

+ Profit margin (markup)

Target ROI Pricing

Set your price at a rate that will achieve a specific Return on Investment target. If you need to make $20,000 from 1,000 units – or $20 per unit – then set your price at $20 more than cost, plus expenses.

Value Based Pricing

This can be a bit of an arbitrary pricing strategy, but it can also be the most profitable. Set your price based on the value or added benefit it brings to a customer. For example, if your product only costs you $40 to produce, but will save the customer $2,000 per year in energy costs, a price of $150 or $200 would not appear to be unreasonable in the eyes of the customer.

Psychological Pricing

What messages are you trying to send the customer when they're looking at your prices for your products? Do you offer the best deal? The highest value? These are reasons to choose prices that are higher or lower than the competition.

Pricing Guidelines

Price higher than cost. This may seem obvious, but ensure that your pricing not only covers your costs, but potential fluctuations in sales volume and in the marketplace. If you sell half of your order, will you still make a profit?

Include expenses. If you price to cover your costs, will you also be able to cover your expenses and still see a profit? Your margin needs to pay for your expenses, leave you with something to live on, plus some working capital for the company.

Consider the 'fair' price. What do your consumers think is 'fair' for each service or product? This is impacted by your competitor's price, your company's image (high quality or high value, low cost), and the perceived value of your product or service.

STRATEGIES TO INCREASE PROFIT

Once you have a concrete understanding of where your business stands today in terms of profitability, minimized operating costs, and restructured pricing strategy, you can focus on other strategies to increase profit.

There are countless strategies and tactics that will help you to bring in more customers, get those customers to come back, and get those customers to spend more when they do.

Here is a list of ideas, many of which are covered in detail in other sections of this program:

- Advertise
- Establish an online presence
- Sell more high margin items
- Generate more leads
- Focus on referral business
- Increase customer loyalty and repeat business
- Increase conversion rates
- Restructure your team
- Reinvent your product
- Sell your intellectual capital

So What Do I Do From Here

✦ ✦ ✦

Get started! Make sure you set your goals. If you do not know where you are going, how can you get there? These goals set the foundation for your business. Ordinary people have accomplished extraordinary things by setting goals and putting into action the steps needed to reach them. By doing so, you are already ahead of 97% of your competition. Next, there are 3 levels in which you can proceed with building you own marketing and sales system.

1) Implement the strategies in this book and track the success of each; and adjust if necessary. Study marketing strategies and develop a desire for proven material. You do NOT have to recreate the wheel. Take successful processes and continue to follow them.

2) Enroll in the Income Generation Academy. By using our proven step by step processes you will expedite the building of your own $50000 plus marketing system for your business.

3) Hire a business coach/consultant as an accountability partner. A good coach will structure their compensation to fit your business's budget, and may base some of their compensation on the results they are able to attain for your business. Remember, larger companies have committees for strategic planning and marketing strategies. You were not meant to have all the answers, and do this alone.

The same thinking that got you where you are today will not get you to the next level. The biggest mistake you can make is to do nothing; or start the process and then fall back into the old habits that will NOT get you to the level you are aspiring to.

There is no Silver bullet, building a successful and valuable business is not difficult, but it does take commitment and hard work. The models for doing so have been created.

To Your Success,

Wayne A. Peterson